The
Bureaucratic
Entrepreneur

The Bureaucratic Entrepreneur

How to Be Effective in Any Unruly Organization

Richard N. Haass

BROOKINGS INSTITUTION PRESS
Washington, D.C.

Copyright © 1999
THE BROOKINGS INSTITUTION
1775 Massachusetts Avenue, N.W.
Washington, D.C. 20036
www.brookings.edu

Library of Congress Cataloging-in-Publication data
Haass, Richard.
    The bureaucratic entrepreneur : how to be effective in any
unruly organization / Richard N. Haass.
    p.   cm.
    Rev. ed. of: Power to persuade.
    Includes bibliographical references.

    ISBN 0-8157-3353-4 (pbk. : alk. paper)
    1. Public administration. 2. Bureaucracy. 3. Performance.
4. Persuasion (Psychology) 5. Office politics. 6. Administrative
agencies—United States—Management. I. Haass, Richard.
Power to persuade. II. Title.
    JF1351 .H2 1999   99-6196
    352.3—dc21   CIP

9 8 7 6 5 4 3 2 1

The Bureaucratic Entreprenuer was first published in 1994 by
Houghton Mifflin as *The Power to Persuade*

The paper used in this publication meets the minimum requirements of the
American Standard for Infomational Sciences—Permanence of Paper for
Printed Library Materials, ANSI Z39.48-1984

Typeset in New Baskerville

Composition by R. Lynn Rivenbark
Macon, Georgia

Printed by R. R. Donnelley and Sons
Harrisonburg, Virginia

To Susan

Note to the Second Edition

It is now five years since the initial publication of *The Power to Persuade*. As the subtitle makes clear, this is a book that provides guidance to individuals who find themselves working in unruly organizations, be they nonprofit or for profit, and regardless of whether they are engaged at the local, state, federal, or international level.

The new edition of the book remains much the same but for three things. The first is the change in title. The original title was derived from Richard Neustadt's classic treatment of the presidency, in which he described the power of the most powerful person in our government as no more than the power to persuade. Alas, the title proved too cryptic for some; hence *The Bureaucratic Entrepreneur*, a title that reflects more precisely what this book is about.

The second change is the addition of considerable new material that reflects the Clinton years. The third and final set of changes is reflected in the additions to the section "Suggestions for Further Reading." For better or worse, there is no shortage of books portraying lessons learned from those who have entered one or another public policy arena.

The original acknowledgment stands. In addition, I would like to thank Candice Geouge, who made sure that the new manuscript kept faith with the original, except where change was intended; Deborah Styles, who edited, and Janet Walker, who coordinated changes to this second edition; and Susan Woollen, who revised the cover for this edition.

RICHARD N. HAASS

Washington, D.C.
April 1999

Acknowledgments

Not surprisingly, there are a good many people to thank, for without them this book never would have come to pass. There are a large number of people in government and at Harvard who taught me by what they said, what they wrote, and, above all, by what they did. I have been blessed over the years by the opportunity to associate and work with a truly gifted bunch of colleagues, bosses, and students.

I owe a major debt to Michael Beschloss, Colin Campbell, Al Carnesale, Susan Mercandetti, Condi Rice, and Ben, Dee, and Liz Sherwood, all of whom read this manuscript in draft, and whose suggestions and criticisms made it far better than it would have been otherwise. My debt extends to Louise Erdmann, who labored mightily to ensure that I not only cited Strunk and White but also applied their precepts to my prose.

I also want to thank those who sat for interviews, who gave of their time and allowed me to violate their privacy and search their memories. Many but not all are mentioned in the book; I do not mention them by name here only because several asked that I not. I would, though, like to mention a number of people—Chris Bosworth, Paul Costello, Vernon Jordan, Ken Kay, Barry Kosofsky, Marty Linsky, Nick Metropolis, Alan MacFarland, Camden McEfee, and Jill Schuker—whose suggestions and phone calls helped make possible many of the interviews that proved so central to this book.

I want to thank the library staff at the Carnegie Endowment for International Peace—Jennifer Little, Chris Henley, and Susan Hanafin—for their frequent assistance in locating one after another obscure book; Liz Jasper, for day in, day out help across the board; and Mort Abramowitz, the president of the Carnegie Endowment, who provided a home for me (along with friendship and counsel) while I worked on this as well as other projects closer to the mission of his institution.

Two other people deserve special mention. The first is my agent, Esther Newberg, who is a real friend and mensch and all around good person despite her support for the Red Sox. (I won't even get into her politics.) The second is my editor, John Sterling, who brought his calm demeanor, keen eye and acute judgment to every page.

RICHARD N. HAASS

Washington, D.C.
November 1993

Preface

You have just had your second cup of coffee. Your pencils are sharpened; your legal pad is at the ready. You may have figured out how to log on to your new computer and done so. You glance at your watch; too soon to start thinking about lunch. You want to succeed, but you are not quite sure what it will take. To be honest, you are not quite sure how to define success.

Sound familiar? This picture of beginning a job is one most of us know well. Few jobs come with a manual describing just what is expected and exactly how to get it done. And even when they do, who wants to do exactly what is expected? Most of us want to leave an imprint, do something that makes a positive difference, do something that gets us some attention and reward.

But how? Where do you go for ideas? How do you figure out what you want to do? Just as important, how do you get it done? How do you cope with demanding bosses and get the most out of subordinates? How do you get along with difficult colleagues and deal with powerful interest groups and the media? Just how do you increase your chances of being effective, exerting influence, and getting ahead?

The answers to such questions are far from obvious. Being effective is difficult. This is true for people in any complex organization; it is especially true for those in government and public-sector jobs, which tend to have overlapping jurisdictions, little autonomy, and multiple constraints. Nonetheless, for many reasons (not always clear), some individuals succeed, while others do not. What is clear, however, is that no two people deal with the challenges in the same way. Not every priest becomes a bishop or cardinal; not all administrators rise to the top position in their school, foundation, or hospital. And few politicians grow up to be president—just as only a fraction of people in business can count on becoming a chief executive officer.

To be sure, talent alone explains why some people do well; there are those who are so smart, and so gifted, that they need no help. Mozart, after all, did not need many music lessons. But this sort of genius is rare. Most of us are more like Mozart's rival Antonio Salieri, good but not great, smart but not brilliant, special but not unique. For us, sheer talent will not suffice. Skills need to be developed. Fortunately, technique can be taught, even if genius cannot.

If I am right, the insights and suggestions in this book will be of use to bosses as well as individuals working in a large government agency or organization, whether they are near the bottom, the middle, or the top. These lessons apply to people working at the federal, state, and local levels and on all topics, from health care and education to defense and transportation. The suggestions may help those in other nonprofit or public sector institutions; they will also benefit those in for-profit enterprises. The good news, as business management authority Peter Drucker has noted, is that "effectiveness can be learned."[1]

By effectiveness, I mean the ability to get the right things done. But what are the right things? Who decides? How do you know if they are correct? Just as important, how do intentions get translated into policies and programs? Answering these and related questions is what this book is about.

The need for increasing the effectiveness of people in complex and often unruly organizations is clear. Some 17 million Americans now work for federal, state, or local government agencies in civilian capacities—nearly as many as work in manufacturing. Moreover, bureaucracies of one sort or another affect us constantly. Government—there are more than 80,000 governmental units at the national, state, and local level—and other public or nonprofit institutions—schools, hospitals, prisons, charities, foundations, churches, and synagogues—affect almost every aspect of our lives. We get educated, healed, taxed, paid, hired, fired, regulated, registered, zoned, licensed, housed, protected, insured, transported, and sometimes drafted by public institutions. Many of us work—full or part time, paid or volunteer—in a public institution. The statistics are telling: Americans belong to more than 22,000 national nonprofit associations. Half of all Americans do volunteer work; 70 percent of U.S. households contribute to one or more charities; and every year 40,000 foundations hand out money.[2]

Despite this involvement, most citizens are not satisfied with the performance of our public institutions. Mention the words "bureaucracy," "civil servant," or "government," and you will almost certainly elicit a negative reaction. These terms conjure up images of inefficiency, waste, or worse. To describe something as "bureaucratic" is pejorative; to call someone a "bureaucrat" is to criticize, to characterize the person as unresponsive, resistant to innovation, and lazy. Putting "bureaucratic" and "entrepreneur" together seems to many people oxymoronic.

It need not be this way. It is hard to imagine that early in the twentieth century the concept of bureaucracy was championed by advocates of good government. It was a welcome innovation, one designed to add professional standards and checks and balances to institutions and processes all too commonly characterized by corruption, spoils, and patronage. But now, bureaucracies often seem to be part of the problem they were meant to solve; one study, for instance, pointed to a "federal performance deficit."[3] All of us have a stake in closing this gap. No democracy can thrive for long amid the perceived failure of its governing institutions, for such failure breeds cynicism, alienation, and, in the end, desperation. Along the way, the best people will choose to leave public service; those who stay will find themselves unable to accomplish what they could and should.

There is no less a need to improve the performance of the millions of Americans working in for-profit businesses of one sort or another. These individuals and the corporations they work for also affect important aspects of our lives, whether we are in the role of employee, neighbor, shareholder, or consumer.

In writing *The Bureaucratic Entrepreneur*, I have drawn on more than two decades of experience in and with a range of organizations. I began as an intern and continued as a legislative assistant in the U.S. Senate. I subsequently served in the Department of Defense, in the Department of State, and on the staff of the National Security Council. I have served on the staffs of four research organizations, consulted for a major television network, and advised several American businesses and corporations in their overseas dealings. I have seen good people accomplish some wonderful things; I have also seen some very good people waste their talents and fail to achieve what was well within their power.

I have also had the chance to think, write, and talk about questions of management. Between stints at the State Department and the White House, I spent nearly four years teaching at Harvard University's John F. Kennedy School of Government. While there, I searched in vain for one book to assign to my students that combined the best of the serious literature of public administration with the personality of memoirs, the insights of case studies, and the pragmatism of many books devoted to effectiveness in the corporate world. This is my attempt to write the book I sought but could not find.

I should note that a number of books and commission reports have appeared over the years devoted to the goal of improving—or "reinventing"—government.[4] Many of the suggestions for what public agencies ought to do—reduce staffing, lessen oversight, repeal burdensome regulations, privatize selected services, end unwarranted subsidies, streamline procurement practices—make a good deal of sense. Some may even get adopted. What such proposed reforms have in common is their aim of increasing *efficiency.*

This book has a very different purpose: it is to increase the *effectiveness* of individuals working in and with governments and other large organizations, including those in the business and corporate worlds. It is designed to help individuals get things done—and by "done" I mean not just approved but implemented—whether or not their government or organization adopts reforms that make them more efficient.

I benefited greatly in writing this book from other people's work: their memoirs, biographies, case studies, textbooks. Many are referred to in the course of the book and in specific notes; those I found especially useful are also listed (and commented on) in the section "Suggestions for Further Reading."

I also conducted more than fifty interviews (excerpts from many of them are scattered throughout the text) with individuals around the United States and in several other countries. Some were former colleagues; some were people I knew of; others were individuals I learned about while writing this book. They were young and old, male and female, civilian and military. They included Asian Americans and African Americans, lobbyists and diplomats, Republicans and Democrats and Independents, elected representatives and civil servants and political appointees. They ranged from the famous to the unknown, from former presidents to junior civil servants. They had experience at the federal, state, and local levels, in the executive branch and in legislatures. Others worked in hospitals, foundations, charities, and universities and for the United Nations and the World Bank. Their specialties ran the gamut—from education and health to the environment and defense. What they had in common was talent, commitment, and an appreciation of what it takes to be effective.

Last, I should preempt my friends and former associates and acknowledge that I intend to preach in these pages what I did not always practice. I made my share of mistakes and then some; I was not always effective. I would like to think that I have learned from my experience. If not, there is the chance that others will, and that they (and we) will be better for it.

Contents

1 Finding Your Way   1

   Designing Your Compass   2
   Why a Compass Helps   3
   The Business of Governing   7
   The Political Landscape   12

2 The Center of Your Compass: You   15

   Getting a Job   16
   Getting Ready   21
   Shaping Your Agenda   23
   Balancing Your Agenda with
      Those of Others   31
   Strengthening the Compass's Center   34
   Conclusions   53

3 **North: Those for Whom You Work**   55

   Before Starting   55
   Adapting to Your Boss   58
   Showing Loyalty Up   63
   Working Successfully with Your Boss   68
   Making Your Case:
      Writing the Persuasive Memo   71
   When to Leave   75
   Conclusions   79

4 **South: Those Who Work for You**   80

   Leading vs. Managing   80
   Transitions   84
   Hiring Choices   87
   Organizing Your Staff   91
   Decisionmaking Choices   96
   Being a Successful Boss   101
   The Boss as Educator   104
   Management Tools   108
   Delegation   110
   Showing Loyalty Down   113
   Letting People Go   116
   Conclusions   117

5 **East: Those with Whom You Work**   119

   Clashing and Cooperating with Colleagues   120
   Seven Rules for Dealing with Colleagues   123
   Turf Wars   125
   Meetings   128
   Chairing Meetings   131
   Ground Rules for Negotiating   133
   Conclusions   143

6   West: Those with Whom You Should Work   145

Why Your West Matters   146
Dealing Effectively with Your West   150
Relations with the Media   155
Legislatures, Councils, and Congress   164
Speaking out in Public   170
Conclusions   175

7   Back to the Center   176

The Five Principles   179

Suggestions for Further Reading   181
Notes   189

1

Finding Your Way

IMAGINE FOR A MOMENT that you are about to set off on a long hike—or, if you prefer, a sailing trip. Few would consider taking a walk through unknown woods or setting out to sea without a compass. It would be reckless, even irresponsible. At the least, it could prove inconvenient; at worst, dangerous.

Making your way through your professional life is no different. For its employees, governments can be dangerous places. So, too, can businesses, schools, foundations, charities, museums, hospitals, and churches. I do not mean physically dangerous (although that cannot be ruled out) so much as dangerous to your professional future, to your personal life, to your welfare, and to your happiness.[1]

Yet many people who work in complex organizations fail to use in their professional lives the navigating tools they would automatically turn to in their personal lives. As a result, they lack direction. They neglect to choose priorities. They never develop strategies and tactics for achieving their goals. When they do set goals, too often they lose sight of them and instead waste effort, make wrong turns, squander opportunities, accomplish little, and do not gain the recognition and reward they could.

Designing Your Compass

Fortunately, just as an actual compass can assist you in the woods or at sea, an imaginary compass can provide direction and guidance in your professional life. Think of your situation at work and imagine that you are holding a compass. Each point of the compass represents a set of critical relationships that must be nurtured and cultivated if you are to be effective. Ignore your compass and you risk getting lost; pay attention to it and you increase the odds that you will determine where you want to get—and get there sooner than you would otherwise.

It is easy to design a compass for the workplace. North represents those for whom you work. To the South are those who work for you. East stands for colleagues, those in your organization with whom you work. West represents those outside your organization who have the potential to affect matters that affect you.

Sketching your own compass is straightforward. My last job in government was as the principal Middle East, Persian Gulf, and South Asia advisor on the National Security Council (NSC) staff. To my immediate North were my boss, Brent Scowcroft, and his deputy Robert Gates, who left after several years to become head of the Central Intelligence Agency (CIA); one step removed to my North was President George Bush. To my South were my deputies, assistants, and secretary. Looking East, I had all my colleagues in the government: my coworkers on the NSC staff and in the White House, at the departments of State and Defense, at the CIA, and at the other executive branch departments and agencies. To my West were all those outside the executive: members of Congress and their staffs, the press, foreign governments and their embassy staffs in Washington, special interest groups, academic experts, and so on.

Another example is the compass of Condoleezza Rice, who is the provost at Stanford University. To her North are the president of the school and the board of trustees; to her South are university employees, the vice provost, and her immediate staff. To her East are the various deans, faculty, and students; her West includes foundations and other sources of funds, alumni, town officials, the press, and parents.[2]

Barry Freedman, the director of a large medical and teaching center in New York City, might design his compass as follows: North are the president of the medical center and the board of trustees; South are doctors, nurses, orderlies, and administrative staff, both individually and through their associations and unions; East are fellow administrators and the dean of the medical school; West includes patients, insurance companies, city, state, and federal officials, regulatory bodies, the community, and the media.

The compass metaphor also works for the world of business. If you work in a for-profit organization, you can easily sketch the points of such a compass: your bosses, employees, and colleagues as well as a host of outsiders, including union leaders, consumers, the press, competitors, and stockholders. Wherever you work, what matters is to identify the individuals and groups most able to affect you and to develop and implement a strategy for working productively with them.

Why a Compass Helps

If navigating your workplace were simple, no compass would be necessary. But being effective in any large organization is difficult, and government and public sector institutions present special problems. First, there is the large number of independent players—officials, legislators and other elected officials, workers and staff of all sorts, interest groups, the media, courts, individual citizens. Then, too, lines of authority are fuzzy, jurisdictions overlap, and philosophies and purposes are at odds with each other.

Accomplishing anything, much less something truly important, in so complex an environment is no mean feat.

Anyone doubting this need only stop for a moment and look around. Many of the principal problems confronting the United States—social security solvency, health care costs and coverage, welfare reform, crime, drugs, unemployment—are incredibly complex. In each case it is hard to know exactly what needs to be done to solve the problem—and harder still to gain public support for doing it. Indeed, in many instances, it is difficult to get a consensus on just what the problem is.

As a result, effectiveness is easier sought than realized. No one is exempt from this reality, not even the president. Just look at Bill Clinton's first few months in office. Republicans in Congress rejected his economic stimulus proposal, and many Democrats balked at his proposed tax increases and spending cuts. The military leadership resisted his proposal to open the armed forces to avowed homosexuals. The same leadership and influential civilians disagreed with the president's belief that the United States should get more involved in the situation in the former Yugoslavia. Two nominees for attorney general were withdrawn; the third, Janet Reno, got the job, but within weeks was involved in a controversial set of decisions that contributed to the deaths of several federal law enforcement agents and scores of members of a religious cult. And on top of all this were political setbacks resulting from the unfortunate symbolism of an expensive presidential haircut aboard *Air Force One,* the clumsy firing of a handful of employees in the White House travel office, and the eleventh-hour withdrawal of a controversial nominee for the post of assistant attorney general for civil rights.

This litany is not designed to single out the Clinton administration for criticism; similar lists could be assembled for its predecessors—and, I am confident, its successors. My point is simple: governing effectively is no easy thing.

This is true for anyone, anywhere. Take Lawrence Walsh, who was appointed independent counsel to investigate the Iran-Contra scandal. Criticized for the slow pace of his prosecutions, Walsh complained about how much was beyond his control. "You're at the mercy of the people who produce the records. You're at the mercy of the witnesses who take their time in deciding to tell you all the facts, and you're at the mercy of the courts who schedule your cases, and who schedule your appeals."[3]

Or consider the metaphors of Charles Frankel, for several years in the mid-1960s the State Department aide in charge of educational and cultural affairs:

> The official has a number of balls in the air. He is engaged in a juggling act. For him, the problem is not the simple one of deciding between doing the right thing and doing the wrong thing. The problem is to decide which of the beautiful balls in the air he will try to catch and which he will allow to fall to the ground. Moreover, the balls he is juggling aren't necessarily balls that he himself has put in the air. Deciding to enter the government is like deciding to marry a girl with a large, old-fashioned family: a man takes on an extensive set of commitments.[4]

Franklin Roosevelt—generally considered one of the most effective presidents—once vented his frustrations with those who supposedly worked for him:

> The Treasury is so large and far-flung and ingrained in its practices that I find it almost impossible to get the action and results I want. . . . But the Treasury is not to be compared with the State Department. You should go through the experience of trying to get any changes in the thinking, policy, and action of the career diplomats and then you'd know what a real problem was. But the Treasury and the State Department are nothing compared with the Na-a-vy. The admirals are really something to cope with—and I should know. To change anything in the Na-a-vy is like punching a feather bed. You punch it with your right hand and you punch it with your left until you are finally exhausted, and then you find the damn bed just as it was before you started punching.[5]

Given such challenges, anything that makes it easier to be effective should be seized on. By "easier" I do not mean less demanding, although it is possible to make a difficult job less or more demanding. Rather, I mean more productive for you. Exerting influence, accomplishing what you want, getting promoted, keeping your personal life intact—these and other objectives are more simple to identify than to achieve.

Nevertheless, some people in large organizations and institutions are able to innovate, effect change, pass legislation, improve performance, save resources, and avoid scandal. But why? Why is it that some people have more influence and are more effective than others? Why do some people get a reputation for getting things done—and, as a result, rise to the top, where others fall or fail?

The answer is not simply that some people are more intelligent; being smart can help, but it is not enough. As Dean Acheson noted, "Brains are no substitute for judgment."[6] Indeed, intelligence can even be a liability if you think that it alone is enough to be effective. It is not just that smart people tend to be intolerant of those less blessed (although they often are). Rather, they tend to believe that by sheer intellectual effort they can come up with the "right" answer and that others will accept this solution and fall into line. The problem, though, is that there rarely is a right answer or a solution that everyone shares. And even on those few occasions when most people do agree, there is no guarantee of results. Even with consensus and the best intentions, there is no assurance that the necessary resources will be available or even that everyone will interpret the decision the same way and translate it into policy as intended.

To succeed in any complex or unruly organization takes a host of qualities. One must push ideas that will withstand scrutiny and be able to persuade others of the appeal of these ideas, then act on them. Thomas Hoving, about to take over the Metropolitan Museum of Art, put it this way: "A director had to be more than a gifted connoisseur, a well-trained scholar, an aesthete, a patient diplomat, a deft fundraiser, an executive, and a conciliator. To be effective—and to survive—the director had to be, in addition, part gunslinger, ward heeler, legal fixer, accomplice smuggler, anarchist, and toady."[7]

Others speak persuasively of the need for versatility. Sir Harold Nicolson, the respected British diplomat and writer, said that the ideal diplomat had to embody "truth, accuracy, calm, patience, good temper, modesty and loyalty." (He took for granted intelligence, knowledge, discernment, prudence, hospitality, charm, industry, courage and tact.)[8] The Czech intellectual and political leader Vaclav Havel cites the necessity of "tact, proper instincts and good taste."[9] Kathleen Sheekey, a former legislative director of Common Cause who went on to become codirector of the Advocacy Institute, suggests that effective people have "a deep commitment to the issue, good substantive knowledge to make their case, and a very good sense of fight." William Safire, a White House speechwriter before he turned syndicated columnist, wrote that aides can choose from a variety of roles: "friend, gadfly, counselor, hatchetman, conscience, philosopher, footstool, amanuensis, spokesman, shoofly, interpreter."[10]

Few of us can claim to personify or possess all these traits. And even if we do not aspire to all of them, it is clear that being effective takes more—a great deal more—than simply being intelligent. The question is exactly what—and how to acquire those skills and put them to good use.

The Business of Governing

Walk into any bookstore, and you are likely to find shelf after shelf of books on business—how to be a better boss, how to be a better manager, how to be a successful leader. There are inspirational stories, how-tos, and case studies. But there are precious few books about government and the public or nonprofit sector, about why some individuals succeed where others fail, and about what can and should be done to make individuals better at governing and managing in the public sector and in other large organizations.

Some people would argue that the books on business are enough, that all we need to do is adapt their precepts for the political world. Indeed, this is a common refrain of those who did well in business: we need to run the government like a business—for what worked in business will work in government—and we will all benefit if this happens. Every now and then a businessman comes along—Ross Perot being but the most recent and visible—who embodies this notion.

Some aspects of business management are indeed making their way into the nonprofit world. For example, Total Quality Management (TQM), a philosophy derived from the writings of management guru W. Edwards Deming, is being introduced into some branches of government. TQM promotes such concepts as teamwork, delegation, a focus on delivering quality to the "customer," and constantly improved processes and procedures. It seems well suited to those agencies that deliver a particular service to large numbers of citizens—for example, motor vehicle licensing, voter registration, entitlement distribution, tax processing, mail delivery. But delivering a service is only one of many things that governments and those in the public sector must do. For most of these other things—improving the quality of education or health care or foreign policy or persuading people outside the organization to go along with some program or policy—TQM and other similar ideas offer only modest assistance.[11]

Understanding why business management precepts tend not to provide much guidance for the public sector requires a quick look at the basic differences between the two worlds. In business, success and failure can be measured and identified by the bottom line: profits. The public sector has no clear equivalent; there is no profit. Rather, performance measures can vary according to ideology and policy preferences. How, for example, does one measure the quality of law enforcement? By the number of arrests? Crime rates? Tickets? Accident rates? Manpower levels? In short, Peter Drucker's question—"What is the bottom line when there is no 'bottom line'?"—is difficult to answer.[12] There is a wide and often unlimited range of policy choice and no agreed on measure for determining efficiency and results. Again, Charles Frankel is worth citing:

> Throughout the American government, there goes on a constant search for "evidence of the effectiveness" of policies. One has to give an answer to this question almost every day to the Bureau of the Budget, Congressional committees or the press. But what *is* evidence? And what does "effectiveness" mean? Is the success of a community action program to be measured by statistical increases in average income? By more votes for the Administration at the next election? By the reduction of militancy in the ghettos? By the increase of such militancy? And what is the span of time within which we are making these judgments—one year, two years, five years? The rules of the game aren't clear.[13]

There are still more important differences. Few businesses enjoy a monopoly; indeed, a purpose of U.S. law since early in the twentieth century has been to limit the ability of any single set of decisionmakers to exert clear control over the marketplace. By contrast, the individual in the nonprofit world is often entrusted with a monopoly. There are not three city administrations for Pittsburgh or multiple boards of election in Topeka competing for your patronage.

Businesses exercise greater freedom in another manner: they can go out of business, or firms can abandon an activity they no longer find profitable.[14] Government rarely has these options, for there are sure to be some powerful groups with an interest in keeping the program up and running. Indeed, there may be social or political value in doing so even if it makes no economic sense; local post offices may not pay their way, but many small towns and the firms based there would suffer enormously from their elimination. Similarly, it is worth noting that the only way to close military bases no longer needed by the Pentagon is to take the decision out of the normal political process and hand it over to a commission granted extraordinary powers.

The very notion of efficiency differs. A business seeks to produce goods or provide services to the potential customer on more attractive terms than those of its rival. Efficiency dictates cutting costs, removing steps, reducing personnel. But the concept of efficiency does not always apply in the public sector, where we may choose to value fairness or a pattern of distributing benefits over concerns about cost or maximizing output.[15] To make this point, the political scientist James Q. Wilson uses the case of New York City's awarding a contract to build a skating rink:

> The economic definition of efficiency (efficiency in the small, so to speak) assumes that there is only one valued output, the new rink. But government has many valued outputs, including a reputation for integrity, the confidence of the people, and the support of important interest groups. When we complain about skating rinks not being built on time we speak as if all we cared about were skating rinks. But when we complain that contracts were awarded without competitive bidding or in a way that allowed bureaucrats to line their pockets we acknowledge that we care about many things besides skating rinks; we care about the contextual goals—the constraints—that we want government to observe. A government that is slow to build rinks but is honest and accountable in its actions and properly responsive to worthy constituencies may be a very efficient government, *if* we measure efficiency in the large by taking into account *all* of the valued outputs.[16]

Anyone who is running a company sees most people as potential or actual consumers. Someone who is involved in running a government or charity sees a citizen in a different light from a consumer. Consumers choose to purchase a specific product or service; by contrast, the citizen's relationship with the "producer" is vague and often involuntary. After all, how many citizens choose to be customers of the Internal Revenue Service, the Social Security Administration, or, in days gone by, their local draft board? And whereas the consumer pays directly and voluntarily for the product or service, the citizen pays indirectly and involuntarily in the form of taxes.

Above all, businesses and the people who work in and for them tend to operate in a more structured, less complex environment. Businesses can set their own goals; they do not have legislatures setting them for them. Businesspeople tend to give and take orders. Decisionmaking is centralized, implementation streamlined. The lines of authority are fairly clear and straightforward; the penalty for violating them is often the loss of one's position. W. Michael Blumenthal, who ran a major company (the Bendix Corporation) and a major government department (he was treasury secretary under Jimmy Carter), describes it graphically:

> In the government no one has the power to decide that this is the policy he wants to develop, these are the people who are going to develop it, this is how it's going to be decided, and these are the folks who are going to administer it. [In a company] you can control the process and tell group executive A, you're not involved, stay out of it. And he will, and he must. In government, that's simply unworkable. So you have to learn to become one of a large number of players in a floating crap game, rather than the leader of a well-organized casino that you're in charge of.[17]

The memoirs of former secretary of state George Shultz include a telling anecdote in which Shultz, a former corporate head, experimented with introducing what worked in business into government.

> I asked Jerry van Gorkom, who had just sold his company to the Pritzker family of Chicago, whether he would like to bring his track record of effective management to Washington and give it a try. He was delighted and accepted. Soon, however, I sensed his frustration. "You've given me this job," he told me one day, and then let loose. "I look over a problem and decide what to do. No sooner have I sent out an instruction than it's overridden by the White

House or leaked to the press, or a call comes in from some congressional staffer irately challenging what we're doing. In business, when we decided to do something, we did it. In government nothing ever gets settled. I can't stand this atmosphere."[18]

Mr. van Gorkom did not last long. He learned the hard way that government and the public sector lack the order, the discipline, the control that many executives take for granted. Actually, if he and his boss had thought about it more, they would not have been surprised by these apparent shortcomings; in fact, our political system was designed to include them.

The Political Landscape

Power in the political world is almost always divided—at times with the explicit purpose of *reducing* efficiency. Just look at the U.S. Constitution. Power is divided among the executive, the legislature, and the judiciary, as well as between the federal government and the states. Unlike the parliamentary system common to most democratic governments, the American system divides the executive branch from the legislative. Richard Neustadt summed it up best in his well-known study of the presidency: "The Constitutional Convention of 1787 is supposed to have created a government of 'separated powers.' It did nothing of the sort. Rather, it created a government of separated institutions *sharing* powers."[19] That this was the intent of the framers is spelled out by James Madison in *Federalist 47*: "The accumulation of all powers, legislative, executive, and judiciary, in the same hands, whether of one, a few, or many, and whether hereditary, self-appointed, or elective, may justly be pronounced the very definition of tyranny." Madison went on to expand his thinking in *Federalist 51*: "Ambition must be made to counteract ambition." The aim was Newtonian, to structure government so that "its several constituent parts may, by their mutual relations, be the means of keeping each other in their proper places."

Few individuals appreciated the balancing of power better than Harry Truman, who had this to say in a letter to his sister in 1947: "The people can never understand why the President does not use his supposedly great power to make 'em behave. Well, all the President is, is a glorified public relations man who spends his time flattering, kissing, and kicking people to get them to do what they are supposed to do anyway."[20] Warming up to his subject, Truman predicted that his successor, Dwight Eisenhower, would encounter real difficulty in moving from the military world of command to the political world of persuasion. "He'll sit right here and he'll say do this, do that! And nothing will happen. Poor Ike— it won't be a bit like the Army. He'll find it very frustrating."[21]

Truman's frustration stemmed from the difference between power and influence. Power is the ability to act or command action, whereas influence is the potential to affect the behavior of those with power. Neustadt, borrowing from Truman, said the power of the American presidency is the power to persuade. He is correct, but his point applies not only to those who occupy the Oval Office, but also to those who occupy offices more traditional in shape. In any environment premised on a distribution of power, monopolies are nonexistent, oligopolies uncommon. The individual can rarely just act, nor is forcing others to act usually an option. The net result is that effectiveness in the political world stems from the ability to influence the people and organizations that share power.

The literature devoted to promoting success in business has thus only limited help for those in the public sector.[22] At the same time, it can be argued that people in business would be wise to consult the literature on politics, as important aspects of a more political environment are making their way into the corporate arena. Management now faces a world over which it has less control, as the former leaders of a good many Fortune 500 firms can acknowledge. Boards of directors, shareholders, the media, courts, workers and unions, regulatory agencies, consumer advocates, environmental and other citizens groups—all now exert growing sway over the corporation. As a result, business leaders are now less free to make their choices and carry them out—and are more accountable—than in the past.

The net result for managers is a loss of freedom, privacy, and control. Traditional techniques for getting work done are no longer adequate. The day of the powerful corporate manager, able to decide in relative isolation his firm's future, confident that his board will support him, the local press will ignore him, and his workers will follow him, is fast fading. As a result, the successful private-sector manager may have to borrow from his public-sector counterpart in order to thrive, even survive. Nowadays, political skills—a functioning compass—are critical for those who operate in the business and corporate worlds, no less than they are for their political counterparts.

2

The Center
of Your
Compass:
You

A COMPASS INDICATES DIRECTION, but it does not tell you where you are. Nor does it tell you where to go. A map, on the other hand, describes an area and gives vital information that can help you decide how to travel from one point to another. By matching what you see with the information provided by the map and the compass, you can orient yourself to learn where you are in relation to where you are going and how to get there.

If you have a map, fine. If not, you can still orient yourself by walking in each direction and looking around. Sooner or later you will have a sense of where you are, what surrounds you, the available paths out—in short, your own mental map. You then have to decide which route to take, how quickly to take it, and so on. No compass or map can choose for you. This must come from within—which is why this chapter addresses you, the center of your compass.

Getting a Job

The first question to ask is the most basic: Do you want a position in the public sector? Participating in events and enterprises that affect us all can be exciting. Government, for better or worse, touches virtually every aspect of our lives. If you get lucky, you can see history being made; if you get even luckier, you can participate in its making. At its best, the public sector offers the opportunity to shape policies that affect the most critical areas of people's lives.

The rewards and satisfaction of public service are evident in the following three accounts. The first comes from Robert Mallett, formerly the city administrator of the District of Columbia.

> It is intellectually challenging to sit in this chair and have sitting there the person from the Corrections Department, the person from the parole board, the person from the Department of Human Services, the person from the AIDS office, and listen to a debate and hear people talk about what kind of policies we ought to have in letting out inmates who may be dying of AIDS or of other diseases in a prison and what impact that has on the prison system. The corrections official says, "We should let these people out as a matter of mercy, but there's also fiscal reasons to do it. I can't afford to do the kind of care in this environment. It's not designed for that." But then listen to the Health Department official who says, "If you let them out they will receive no health care." And then you hear the mother of one of the inmates say, "Don't let him out. I know you're trying, but it's not merciful to do that. I can't handle it.". . . You can't listen to that debate, you can't be a part of it, and not be very emotionally drained and very intellectually challenged.

Ralph Neas was, for more than a decade, the executive director of the Leadership Conference on Civil Rights, one of this country's most influential public interest coalitions. He tells this story about himself when he was leaving Congress, where he had toiled as an aide:

After I left Senator David Durenberger's office, he, Senator Edward Brooke, and many others advised me to join a law firm and start becoming financially independent. They made all the legitimate arguments that my father and mother had been making for some time. And there's no question that by far the majority view among my close friends was, "Don't go with the Leadership Conference on Civil Rights. Go back to a law firm or go somewhere else in the private sector." However, there were a number of people, including John Sears, the conservative Republican, who counseled me to go with the Leadership Conference. [He argued that] there would only be so many opportunities in my life to be part of history. He said, "You and I don't agree on civil rights issues, and believe me, Ronald Reagan and the people I know who are coming into power don't believe anything you believe. But if you become the Director of the Leadership Conference, you will be a leader of an organization that will be trying to prevent them from undermining what you have always believed in and have been part of and have been in part responsible for. And if I were you, I would not pass up the opportunity to be on the front lines in this great battle, whether it's for two years, four years, six years, whatever. It will be fun. It will be challenging. And you'll never regret seizing this opportunity."

Elizabeth Reveal, for a time Seattle's finance director, has held similar jobs in other cities, including Philadelphia:

I gave the keynote speech at a business community meeting for Wharton [the University of Pennsylvania's business school]. I was the first public-sector person that they ever had do this, and I sat next to a guy who runs huge municipal mutual funds and who told me all about his work. He said, "What do you do?" I said, "Well, I am Chief Financial Officer of a four-billion-dollar corporation and we are very diversified on everything from solid waste disposal to long term care. And I do about $2 billion a year of debt and I manage a $4 billion pension fund and procure about $2 billion a year.

It's very diverse, very interesting, and I make $80,000 a year."
And he looked at me and he said, "What! I bet you don't even
have a house in the Hamptons." A house in the Hamptons! I
can't afford a house in Philly. But when you think about it,
there is no institution, really few institutions on earth, that
are as diverse, as complex, as politically and legally and policy
challenging, as a big city government.

For young people, government has an additional attraction. At
an early age, and with relatively little experience, you can often find
yourself involved in important undertakings and assuming considerable responsibility. I remember a friend of mine from graduate
school—Richard Sauber—who, after completing law school,
entered the Justice Department. He soon found himself heading a
small task force empowered to investigate and prosecute energy
companies that were violating certain pricing guidelines in effect
in the early 1980s. One of the cases went to trial; he, not yet thirty,
was behind one table, while a defense team of a dozen lawyers
(some of whom were twice his age) sat on the other side of the
courtroom. The defense lawyers who were his age were doing little
more than carrying briefcases. And this was no exception—just
look at the young age of many of the staff serving your senator or
president. Opportunity can knock in the public sector far sooner
than elsewhere.

The public sector can also provide excellent opportunities for
women and minorities. Almost all of the women I interviewed for
this book commented on the relative absence of discrimination
and the relative abundance of opportunity. John Payton, formerly
Washington, D.C.'s counsel, has this to add about opportunities
for African Americans:

> Probably for most of the lawyers who work here, this will be
> the only job they'll ever have where their senior manager is
> black. And where the senior management team, if there are
> eight deputies, four are white, four are black. It changes
> some expectations and dynamics, but in our relations we
> work out just great. And that itself is reassuring and empow-

ering to an awful lot of people. The problem that drives reality in a law firm is you have to generate business. You don't have to generate business here. All you have to do is do a good job for the clients, be able to deal with disputes across agencies, work out this problem. I can define what it is you have to do. The best part? It is within your control. A judge can act unfairly, and therefore you may not get a result you want, but you won't be blamed for that. I appreciate that. How you do your job? That's up to you. That's within your control. That is why a lot of black people feel more comfortable in that kind of setting, because they're not judged by something that is completely beyond their control.

There are, nevertheless, obvious downsides to a career in government and the public sector. There is a good deal more hard work and anonymity than glamour or fame. It is often frustrating. Getting things done is hard; measuring what you have accomplished is often impossible, given the absence of relevant yardsticks. It can get tough in terms of criticism and thin in the way of praise. You will find yourself defending in public decisions you opposed in private. The pay often compares poorly with the private sector; the hours can be long. The job can lead to legal problems. And your life is not your own: you can expect drug testing, financial disclosure requirements, and strict conflict-of-interest rules that can limit your options, not just while you have your job, but for years to come. You are never off duty, and the media consider you fair game for what you say and do both in and out of the office.

The demands of many public-sector jobs exact a heavy toll on personal lives. The description of what happened in less than one year to Howard Paster, Bill Clinton's chief legislative lobbyist, is sobering. "During his long hours, the chief lobbyist lay awake on many nights. He had stopped exercising, was eating more junk food, and was gaining weight. His ingestion of Diet Coke, always impressive, grew to be prodigious; he bought the stuff by the case. And a stress-related rash forced him to visit a dermatologist—twice."[1]

Families also suffer. Sheila Burke, who is married and has three children, worked with Senator Robert Dole for sixteen years, half of that time as his chief of staff. The tradeoffs are clear:

> You can't ever not feel guilty. You're always guilty. You're guilty when you leave for work and you're guilty when you get home. Somebody, somewhere, is paying a price. You just have to watch your own children and see how they behave. There are times when I sense that the kids are more anxious than at other times, and I will consciously just make a decision to spend more time with them. There are times when I know I cannot, and I'll just say to my spouse, "I've just got to not be there for whatever it is." . . . These are not jobs for people who are faint-hearted. These are jobs for people who are willing to commit that kind of time. That's it. If I was somebody who was going to be overwhelmed with guilt because I wasn't home every single night for dinner, this would not be the right job, and I would have had to acknowledge that years ago.

Robert Reich, secretary of labor during Bill Clinton's first term, expresses the tradeoffs no less poignantly. "How do you balance a job you're deeply committed to against a family you deeply love? In the end, you can't. It's not a matter of finding a better 'balance' because you can't do more of *both*. It's not fixed by managing your time better because you can't schedule when a young teenager will want to sit and talk, or when you and your spouse will want to share intimacies."[2]

In my most recent government job, I made a sacrifice of a different sort. I was married in November 1990, several months after the Iraqi invasion of Kuwait. I arrived in Boston late on a Friday, just in time for the rehearsal dinner, got married on Saturday, attended a brunch on Sunday, and left for Paris on Monday. But it was hardly a honeymoon. When I flew to Paris I traveled alone, to join President Bush on a trip to the Persian Gulf to visit U.S. and allied troops over Thanksgiving. By the time I got around to taking a honeymoon the next April, I had the challenge of explaining in my pidgin French just why I was honeymooning with a woman five months pregnant.

Getting Ready

There are many ways of getting a job in the public sector. You can try the obvious routes of applying directly to the civil service, the foreign service, or the military. Or you can work on a campaign and hope that your side wins and you get rewarded. You can become an expert and build a reputation that attracts an offer. You can hitch your wagon to someone more senior—a mentor—and hope that he or she gets lucky and takes you along. Connections can help, but rarely are enough. Even if they get you in the door, you will find yourself going the other way unless you perform.

Knowing what job to pursue—or, if you are lucky, which to accept—is not as easy at it sounds. You need to ask what exactly you have to offer. It makes no sense to aim too high if your qualifications are inadequate or if you have little or no experience in the field that interests you. Since it is often easier to move up from within, it can make sense to accept a job that gets you in the door even if the move is horizontal rather than vertical. Consider what you need and want at this stage in your career. When I was younger, I took some jobs—internships and positions with minimal salaries—for the experience. I wanted to learn more about government and get a feel for how policy was made. Only later in life did I ask tougher questions about whether I would enjoy enough access and influence to justify the inevitable sacrifices.

Preparing for a new job is no easy matter. There is no substitute for good communication skills—above all, the ability to write. You can pick up the substance of what you are doing more quickly than you can the ability to write well. That said, having some kind of background in a field related to the job is always useful. A sense of perspective and history is invaluable, especially since you are unlikely to have much opportunity to study history once you are there. Most jobs tend to keep you too busy.

The question of education is also worth addressing. Some people believe that legal training is valuable even if you do not plan to practice law or provide legal advice. They stress the discipline and rigor that legal training can provide. This is a sensible notion, but three years and tens of thousands of dollars is not an option for everyone; also, I am not convinced that legal training is always the best background for dealing effectively in an environment where influence and personality matter as much as if not more than rules.

Graduate schools and programs in public policy and public administration, which are proliferating, offer another route. These programs—more like business schools than schools of law or medicine or engineering, which teach bodies of knowledge—emphasize analytical skills and a sprinkling of management courses rather than developing expertise in any particular realm. The ability to perform quantitative analysis can be valuable, especially if you find yourself negotiating resource levels or debating the merits of competing proposals with someone who has this technical skill. But such a focus on skills is no substitute for either specific knowledge of a subject or actual experience. Again, it is debatable whether this general professional preparation is for everyone, given its cost in both time and resources.[3]

Regardless of your formal educational background, you will want to take time before you start a job to "read in," to learn the lay of the land in your new field. Your research can range from a trip to the library and reading a few books to surfing the Internet or perusing the daily newspaper and trade or specialty publications. You want to do this not simply to make a good impression or to make it easier to get up to speed, but also to help you figure out what needs to be done. Far too many people put much or all of their energy into getting a position or getting elected—and neglect to prepare themselves for what they want to accomplish once there, as though they are content to *be* the job rather than *do* it.

Shaping Your Agenda

Everyone who works effectively in the public sector has a personal agenda, a set of goals and priorities that must be developed. You have to tailor one for yourself, based on your values and beliefs and your life experience. Ideas matter. A good many policies and innovations begin as someone's inspiration. At the same time, an agenda should reflect your personal situation, including where you are in your career, what you want out of the job, the nature of the job, and the political context—your boss's agenda, the mandate and platform of the relevant elected official, the resources available, and the overall political balance between and among parties, institutions, and interest groups. Thus you can and should define what you want to achieve —issues and changes you want to effect— but these ambitions must be tempered by the circumstances— opportunities and constraints alike—in which you find yourself. You will want to talk to others before setting your agenda. You need to confer with your boss, because certain limits may have been set for you. Spending some time with your predecessors and the incumbent you are about to replace is always a good investment. Just as important is speaking to people already active in the field: experts, new colleagues, interest groups, your staff. Everyone is a potential resource.

Other considerations can help. You cannot achieve everything, certainly not at the same time. There are only so many hours in the day, only so many issues that any person can be an expert on, only so much access that you can enjoy, only so many decisions that an organization can make. Priorities matter; sequence, too, can be terribly important. The key is to focus—something that takes real discipline, since in a typical day you might be confronted with more than a dozen issues, as many phone calls, several meetings, and inches of paper to read.

This need to specialize, to focus, is one of the keys to effectiveness. One former senior White House official explains the need to keep your agenda narrow:

I used to have a rule for myself that at any point in time I wanted to have in mind—as it so happens, also in writing, on a little card I carried around with me—the three big things I was trying to get done. Three. Not two. Not four. Not five. Not ten. Three. Now, it's a somewhat arbitrary number. The reason it's important to go through an exercise to find three—and I really think the process degenerates when you start going up to four, five, six, seven, based on having played around with this for many, many, many years—the reason it's important to come up with some number like three, a small number, is that there are so many opportunities for distraction, so many ways in which you can spend your time, all of which seem important, and where the claimants feel intensely that they are important, that if you have not gone through some process to identify "the three," you may well end up with zero. You will have accomplished nothing. You could spend a tremendous amount of time seeming to be busier than in any other walk of life, working on extraordinarily important things, without getting anything of real consequence done. So you have to come up with your set of a big three. And every single day, at the start of the day, ask, "What am I doing to advance the big three?" Have a little check list. You've got to be disciplined or else the distractive opportunities and influences will overwhelm you.

This view of the necessity of maintaining your focus is echoed by William Kristol, formerly chief of staff to Vice President Dan Quayle:

You need to realize the paradox of politics. If you are not on offense, you are on defense. It's easier to ride a bicycle going faster than going slowly or standing still. And therefore, if you don't make your own news and create your own momentum, others will make the news about you. There's no such thing as a time out. There's no such thing as let's do nothing . . . if you don't have two or three goals, you will be buffeted by this, this, this and this . . . it will lead you to reacting to a zillion things.[4]

To some extent, what you seek to achieve must relate not simply to yourself but to the position. Some jobs offer a chance to affect grand policy; others, only to influence some small piece of how a policy is implemented. It is usually a waste of effort to fight your situation; instead, you should assess its strengths and make the most of them. A classic example is what William Bennett did at the Department of Education, an agency that controls only some 6 percent of what is spent in this country on education. Bennett decided that he could do the most by using his position as a bully pulpit, that his principal tools were ideas and words rather than programs and resources. So he focused on speeches and meetings with those in a position to command resources. Similarly, C. Everett Koop as surgeon general used his office more as a means of shaping the public debate and thinking about major health-related issues than as an opportunity for effecting specific reforms.

Morton Abramowitz, who held no fewer than thirty-one jobs in government over a career spanning some three decades, spent four of those years in the mid-1980s as the assistant secretary of state for intelligence and research (INR). His description of his attempt to be influential (and where not to focus) illustrates well how to exploit the strengths—and take into account the limitations—of your position:

> If you focus on an issue which is not a first rung issue, but a second rung issue, and have a very decided point of view, and you have access to senior individuals, you can do a lot. On almost any issue that was being dealt with, there was somebody else who knew more about it than I did. So I had to find ways to make INR something different. So I was always looking for approaches, for issues that we could be different on. One reason we could be different on Afghanistan and Iran is that there were no embassies there. There was nobody reporting. We controlled the major thing, which was intelligence. On hostage issues, the other bureaus couldn't reach us, they couldn't touch us. Playing to your strengths was the nature of the business.

These comments underline another key factor that should affect your agenda. How many other people are pushing or likely to push issues in the area you are contemplating? You want to make sure the field is not too crowded before you enter, unless you are convinced that there is a real opportunity to accomplish something and that you are in the best position to do so. Giandomenico Picco, for years a top official at the United Nations, more than anyone else helped bring about the release of the American hostages in Lebanon. He told me he chose an issue to focus on (he chose just four in a twenty-year career) only if he was well-positioned, had an idea of what to do, and saw a vacuum.

You also have to judge the times and the political environment. You can only fight on so many fronts at once, and some causes are more likely than others to be winnable. Issues have a way of ripening, of evolving to a point where political action can have a constructive impact. We have seen it recently with both the deficit and health care. There are a number of telltale signs: usually an issue and possible initiatives to address it are being discussed by policy elites, and there is mounting popular support for some sort of action.

Sometimes an event can create an opportunity. I was working in the Pentagon in the late 1970s, when the fall of the Shah of Iran and the Soviet invasion of Afghanistan increased interest in the Persian Gulf area. We turned our focus to U.S. forces and plans for that region, and before long the Rapid Deployment Force, the precursor of the Central Command that won the 1990–91 Gulf war, was born. But quick reflexes are important: as John Kingdon points out, "Policy windows open infrequently, and don't stay open long."[5] You need to be alert to them—and adjust your agendas accordingly. Indeed, unexpected developments can be a double-edged sword. In some cases they can be opportunities; in others, events can prove constraining. Many a chief executive has been frustrated by a sudden budget crisis or unexpected scandal. Or imagine yourself in the shoes of Tom Sawyer, currently a congressman from Ohio, who became mayor of Akron just two days after the city's chief power plant shut down because of explosions—leading to a major loss of both revenue and heat for much of Akron. In such circumstances, your agenda is all but set for you. But this is the exception.

What you set out to do should also be within reach. It makes little sense to establish as your goal "world peace" or "the elimination of the underclass." Something grand and fairly general might be appropriate for your mission statement—Richard Riley's Education Department is committed to ensuring "equal access to education and to promot[ing] educational excellence throughout the nation"—but this is not to be confused with objectives, much less proposals or programs. Your mission and broad objectives need to be broken down into something more modest and concrete. Similarly, you need to be sure that you define the issue correctly. Again, Kingdon is worth listening to: "There is a difference between a condition and a problem. . . . Conditions become defined as problems when we come to believe that we should do something about them."[6] To this I would only add that you must also believe that you *can* do something about a problem: intentions must always be grounded in capacity if you are to do more than tilt at windmills.

The former White House aide who suggests limiting your goals to three argues for even greater precision when it comes to calculating the chance they will be adopted:

> I tried to find things that were very big, that most reasonable people would say that if you got that done, that would be a very big thing, a very important thing, but where it was not likely to happen on its own, but where the probability of success was not so low that you were wasting your time. Now, what probability does it need to be? That's hard to judge, but I think it's got to be in the range of .3 to .6. If it starts to get too much above .6, it's going to happen without you anyway. If it drops too much below .3, you're probably being a little quixotic. . . . It isn't that you should say I'll never work on

issues that are very low probability, but if they have very low probabilities, you've got to have a fairly long time horizon and be planning to work on them rather intermittently. They shouldn't be on your big three list until they're a little riper.

The notion of choosing goals that stand a chance of being realized is critical. Sometimes this means scaling back your ambitions. Kathleen Sheekey, a proponent of long-shot causes at both Common Cause and the Advocacy Institute, makes the realist's case:

> Having winnable goals is very important. Sometimes that in turn has to be broken down into small steps. . . . So, in 1986, when Senator [David] Boren said in the Senate, I'll introduce an amendment to limit the amount of PAC [Political Action Committee] money any senator can take, that was far from what Common Cause wanted in terms of comprehensive campaign finance reform—Common Cause had always said that limitations without public financing and overall spending limits were not what they wanted—but that was the only game in town that year. It was a good first step. So we put our weight behind that amendment. It passed. That was a winnable goal.

Sometimes you can increase the chances that something new will be accepted if you make it small to begin with. As a study published by the Council for Excellence in Government has noted, "Useful innovation often comes in small packages."[7] Ellen Schall, who served as commissioner of New York City's Department of Juvenile Justice, speaks of "chunking" the work.

> The expectations of public-sector service agencies are enormous and potentially overwhelming. For example, telling staff that their responsibility is to eliminate juvenile delinquency, even for a limited group of citizens, is to invite chaos or collapse. The task is just too overwhelming. Thus the manager has the responsibility to organize the work so that staff have clear, reachable milestones—specific objectives that can be identified and achieved. . . . By selecting a concrete and

available goal and "chunking" the work into doable pieces, agency leaders make success both clearer and nearer. And they create opportunities for staff to get recognized for their work and accomplishments.[8]

Taking small steps can have other advantages. Supporters are pleased that a precedent has been established and a framework created; opponents (or at least skeptics) are pleased that the initial commitment is modest in scale. Skeptics can be further assuaged if a mechanism for evaluation is built in and if pauses in implementation are scheduled to allow for any necessary adjustment—features that backers ought to welcome, too, as opportunities to improve the program and thereby gain support for its continuation and expansion. This is very much what emerged in 1993 from the debate over the Clinton administration's proposal for national service: the pilot program gave advocates something to point to, but it was small enough not to scare off those who feared its potential cost.[9]

Your goals need not be positive. In some circumstances, it may be wise to build your agenda at least in part around the objective of thwarting the agendas of others. Such an approach is not a substitute for having something you want to accomplish, but it can be a complement. As a general rule, it is easier to block than it is to build; the Constitution raises this to a principle by providing for presidential vetoes and making it difficult for Congress to override them. Indeed, a "negative" agenda (or, more precisely, a negative portion of an agenda) may be appropriate for those in the minority or for a chief executive faced with a legislature controlled by the opposition. Roger Porter, who was a senior aide to President George Bush, puts forth the merits of a "blocking" agenda:

> I think Bush stopped a number of bad things from happening. He exercised his veto power more frequently than his predecessor. He exercised it more successfully than any of his predecessors. One of the little appreciated facts was that you were able to stop certain things from happening that could

be counter-productive. It is hard to go out and trumpet that as a great achievement, but in fact anybody who has worked inside government knows that you are not only trying to make good things happen but you are trying to prevent bad things from happening. . . . People don't adequately appreciate that you may come to the end of the day and feel good because you got something that was going off the road back on the road, that you stopped something from going off on a detour, as opposed to being able to say that you advanced the ball down the field.

Finally, your agenda can and normally should evolve as you stay in the job. Little is ever static, and your agenda ought to change as new opportunities come along. This is not an argument for giving up—perseverance is one of the chief attributes of effective people—but only for recognizing that you and the context you are working in are likely to change, and that as they do, you should reassess what it is you are trying to accomplish. John Danforth, a former U.S. senator from Missouri, reveals how agendas should evolve:

You have to have, necessarily, a limited number of things you are doing. You can't do everything at once. In this particular job, there are unlimited demands on how you can spend your time. You can go to every single hearing on your schedule card. You can speak on every amendment to every bill that's on the floor of the Senate. You can answer all of your mail personally. There are senators around who have large staffs to hold their hands. They are just forever reading memos and signing their own mail and on and on, and I often wonder how they can manage to do that. It's very important to have a finite number of things that you do. Now, did I on day one in the Senate, after the 1976 election, sit down and say, "Alright, here are three finite things that I want to do and then stick with those over the next sixteen-plus years?" The answer to that is no. Interests change, interests evolve, things come up, you change as a person, what's important to you changes.

Balancing Your Agenda with Those of Others

To this discussion of agendas I would add one last—but critical—point. As noted earlier, agendas must come from within, but they must also take account of circumstances. It is always a good investment of both time and effort to try out possible goals on those who constitute your compass—your boss, your staff, your colleagues, and outside groups and organizations. This is the best way to gain, test, and improve ideas, to shape them so they can be adopted and then implemented efficiently. It is essential to interact with all the points of your compass; the people who pay attention to only the center of their compass will have no better success than those who ignore the center altogether and do only what others want.

Clearly a balance must be struck between listening to yourself—pursuing your desired agenda—and listening to others—modifying your agenda to gain necessary support. The individual who gets too far out in front of others will wind up alone and without influence. But one who only listens, who only does what people around him desire, will make no mark. Such a person will be led rather than lead.

If you want to make a mark, there is no substitute for fashioning your own framework, your own operating philosophy. This philosophy—which reflects your core beliefs and your view of people, society, and the world—provides the intellectual and moral foundation for an agenda. It pushes you in a defined direction; others will then react to you, you will react to them, and over time your agenda will be refined. This is why no point on the compass is more important than the center; no point can provide direction unless you first decide where it is you want to go. You can only persuade others to follow if you know where you are going.

Developing an operating philosophy requires experience, study, and plain hard thought. The life of Ralph Neas, a powerful advocate of civil rights, is a testament to how philosophy comes to reflect all that you have been exposed to:

I've always wondered exactly when I first started learning about civil rights issues. I'm sure in part it was from my family; in part it was from the teachings of the Catholic Church. Notre Dame, especially its president, Father Ted Hesburgh, certainly played a role. And my long bout with Guillain-Barré Syndrome without question broadened my understanding of such issues and reinforced my commitment. But I believe that among the most important influences were the kinds of books that I read as a child and the type of personal experiences I had growing up. I loved political biographies, especially those about Abraham Lincoln. I found the accounts of slavery and other forms of unconscionable discrimination and the efforts to eliminate them fascinating.

The views of former Massachusetts governor William Weld on social questions—in this case, his approach to the controversial issue of abortion—reflect his upbringing and personal experience more than anything academic or political.

I hate being preached at by the government. I don't mind being preached at by a preacher, because that's the assumption of the risk if you go sit in a congregation. You can expect to be preached at. But a preachy tone out of the government is just not something I care for at all. I'm a real Yankee, a real "Don't tread on me" northern type. That may be where that comes from. What really brought it home to me [was] the abortion issue. My wife and I have five kids. One of them was a slight problem during the pregnancy, and the doctors sort of thought it maybe would be a handy, convenient idea to terminate this pregnancy. We absolutely wouldn't hear of it. Which was fine, that was our decision. But if someone had said, we should consult our local legislator about whether this was a good idea, I would have looked at them as though they were a space creature.

Kim Beazley, the leader of the Australian Labor party, has this to say on where you get your philosophy—and on the importance of having one:

It takes a long time. It comes from your gut. It comes from your experiences of life. It comes from the way you were educated. It comes from your own analysis of the nature of your society. You have to be prepared to have a daily interaction between the philosophical and the real. If you don't allow for that, you become a lunatic. You're just a crazed participant in the political system. That's something you have to comprehend. But the penalty of not having a philosophy is a total lack of direction, getting easily bogged down, and atrophy.

Sometimes, however, you can have too much philosophy, and beliefs cross the line into ideology. Individuals who are unable to listen, unable to adapt to the political environment, are heading for trouble. They will either alienate the people in their compass points and fail to gain support for their ideas, or they will try to ignore their political environment and lose legitimacy in a vain effort to overcome resistance. Either way, effectiveness will plummet. Capable people realize that only by interacting with other centers of power inside and outside of the organization can ideas take hold.

Sir Isaiah Berlin, in his famous essay on the hedgehog and the fox, differentiates between two types of intellects and personalities found throughout history.[10] The hedgehog tends to know one thing and one thing only; his is the worldview that explains everything. The strength of this approach is the consistency and confidence it yields. The danger, of course, is that it leads to blindness when facts do not accord with the ideology and to an intolerance of those who hold a different world view. The opposite of the hedgehog is the fox, who darts from issue to issue without bias, seeing everything on its own merits, everything as unique. The advantage is open-mindedness and a willingness to consider new ideas; the downside is that the fox often lacks direction and risks making little forward progress despite all his exertions.

Effectiveness is maximized when we are part hedgehog, part fox. Effective people will take initiatives, make decisions, even take risks, but will work with others at all phases of the enterprise and will modify their actions when others pose good ideas or when it is necessary to change course in order to gain support for part of what is sought. The relationship among philosophy, agenda, and compass is thus critical. Philosophy reflects your worldview, but an agenda, while being consistent with your philosophy, must also be tailored to the political environment. Interacting with the points of your compass is how this tailoring takes place.

Strengthening the Compass's Center

Once you have determined what you want to accomplish, write it down on a piece of paper and put it in your desk drawer. Review it every few months to see how you are doing and whether the list is still appropriate and adequate. Update it if need be, although if you add something new, you should probably subtract something old. Fighter pilots never forget one maxim: "Keep your eye on the bubble." The "bubble" is the cockpit instrument (much like a carpenter's level) that shows the relationship between the pitch of the aircraft and the horizon. For a pilot, losing sight of the bubble can be the difference between life and death; for the individual working in government or in any complex organization, losing sight of priorities can be the difference between being effective and being forgotten.

Much of what you can accomplish will depend on how you deal with those who work at the four points of your compass—the subjects of the next four chapters. But there are ways to help yourself once you have thought about what you want to accomplish. Some of these guidelines may seem trivial, but remember that God (or the devil) is in the details.

Pledge Yourself to Excellence

Here I can do no better than to quote the business writer Mark McCormack: "Commit yourself to quality from day one. Concentrate on each task, whether trivial or crucial, as if it's the only thing that matters (it usually is). It is better to do nothing at all than to do something badly."[11] Never accept the cynical notion that something "is good enough for government work." Better yet, try to transform the phrase. Just as "Made in Japan" evolved in one generation from connoting cheapness to connoting quality, your goal should be to make people view "government work" as a standard of excellence.

Pledging yourself to excellence means worrying about the little things. Details matter. Let former Baltimore Oriole baseball manager Earl Weaver be your guide: do the little things well and you won't have to do the extraordinary quite so often. Or, borrowing again from the world of sports—in this case, Atlanta Falcons football coach Dan Reeves—remember that "the difference between winning and losing is doing things right and doing things exactly right."[12]

Nothing is too small. William G. Pagonis, the general in charge of logistics during Operations Desert Shield and Desert Storm, relates the following story of how nothing can be taken for granted:

> General [Norman] Schwarzkopf . . . had contacted my office to complain about the shortcomings of our heavy desert uniform, and particularly about the desert boot that we were then distributing to our troops. The boots had been designed for combat in Vietnam, where buried booby traps had posed a serious threat to soldiers. In that era, therefore, a metal plate had been incorporated in the sole of the boot, providing nearly complete protection against pungi-stick traps. But what is a boon in the jungle may turn out to be a curse in the desert, where the extreme heat of the sand—say, at midday in August—would heat up the plate in the soldier's shoe, and consequently badly burn his or her feet.[13]

Pledging yourself to excellence also means being sufficiently honest to change your position or policy as new facts and arguments come to light. Listen to what John Magaw, the secret service agent who took over the Bureau of Alcohol, Tobacco and Firearms in the aftermath of the 1993 Waco, Texas, debacle, has to say: "One of the key things we've learned is that it's never to late to call something off. It's never too expensive or embarrassing to stop an operation if we think it won't work."[14] The moral is clear: never allow pride or arrogance to prevent you from doing what seems right.

Never Assume Anything

Murphy's Law—anything that can go wrong will—remains in effect. In his seminal study *On War,* Carl von Clausewitz writes of "friction," a concept akin to chance, the inevitable byproduct of people's interacting with one another and with events. Substitute the word "politics" for "war," and the relevance of Clausewitz's insight will be apparent.

> Everything in war is very simple, but the simplest thing is difficult. . . . Imagine a traveler who late in the day decides to cover two more stages before nightfall. Only four or five hours more, on a paved highway with relays of horses: it should be an easy trip. But at the next station he finds no fresh horses, or only poor ones; the country grows hilly, the road bad, night falls, and finally after many difficulties he is only too glad to reach a resting place with any kind of primitive accommodation. It is much the same in war. Countless minor incidents—the kind you can never really foresee— combine to lower the general level of performance, so that one always falls far short of the intended goal. . . . Friction is the only concept that more or less corresponds to the factors that distinguish real war from war on paper.[15]

Another war-related story comes to mind here. Just days after Iraq invaded Kuwait, the Bush administration had secured Saudi Arabia's approval for what became Operation Desert Shield, the plan for deterring an Iraqi attack on (and, if need be, defending) Saudi Arabia. This in turn required that we get necessary overflight rights and basing support. We wanted it done quietly, lest

THE CENTER OF YOUR COMPASS: YOU 37

we alert Iraq to our intent at the moment of our maximum military vulnerability. The decision was made to limit any communication of our plans to only the highest levels, to those with a real need to know. Sitting in the Situation Room in the White House basement, I was feeling confident until I discovered a cable, sent out by a sergeant at McGuire Air Force Base in New Jersey, alerting just about the entire world to our plans. He was simply following standard operating procedure (SOP) for disseminating such cables; so much for keeping the decision and the movements of our forces quiet.

Another example of Murphy's Law at work took place one day late in 1990. The U.S. policy toward Lithuania had become quite controversial—the Bush administration was accused of not doing enough for the Lithuanians in their struggle against Moscow's authority. The Lithuanian prime minister was invited to the White House, but when she arrived, the gate would not open. Some mechanical gremlin had struck. The prime minister was forced to get out of her car and walk up the long driveway—all in front of a press corps that was convinced this was a planned snub. When the gate opened normally an hour later for the Jamaican prime minister, it only made matters worse.

Sometimes—as in the last example—nothing can be done to prepare for the unexpected and unprecedented. But in other situations you can do a number of things to protect yourself from Murphy's Law. Just because you sent something does not mean it arrived. Better to check up (or have someone do it for you) than to learn later that something was not done because it fell through the cracks. Or, in the case of the mis-sent cable, we would have been wise to ensure that special rather than standard procedures were in effect, given the high stakes.

Sometimes it is worth taking extraordinary care to limit your vulnerability to Murphy's Law. When Bill Clinton stood before the country on September 22, 1993, to deliver his address on health care, he was shocked to see the text of his State of the Union address in the TelePrompTer. The impact of Clinton's appeal on this major issue could have been measurably diminished if he had not been able to use the TelePrompTer. The day was saved by David Dreyer, a White House aide, who carried with him not only an extra copy of the speech but an extra computer disk, which he inserted into the TelePrompTer. This is what being prepared is all about.[16]

Do Not Be Afraid to Act

I am not suggesting that you be impulsive, much less reckless, but at some point—after you have read or heard the relevant arguments and considered them carefully—further debate and reflection become marginal and delay becomes a de facto decision to do nothing. Philip Lader, previously deputy director in charge of management in the Clinton administration's Office of Management and Budget, now U.S. ambassador to Great Britain, argues for bringing Nike's advertising slogan to government:

> [People] should be prepared, like the little Dutch boy, who was willing, when he saw a hole in the dike, to stay up all night, plug it with his finger, and thereby save his country. It can be argued that anybody could have done that, but he was the one who saw the need, was willing to sacrifice, and actually did it. And maybe that is the lesson of public management: be prepared, be willing to sacrifice, and just, at some point, to do it. . . . At some point, the navel-gazing and the quantitative analysis only lead to a paralysis. And often times, after you have brought the best intellectual resources and the most experienced practical minds to it, you've got to just do it.

A related maxim is not to let papers gather dust in your in-box. Janet Hale, once a senior official in the Office of Management and Budget, offers this blunt perspective on her job: "It didn't do any good to let the decisions very often sit there in some aging process. We weren't making wine; we were making laws and regs [regulations]. We tried to push them along rather than just bury them."

Make it your aim to accomplish things, not to avoid criticism. Some of the most depressing words I ever read were written by an anonymous government official and appeared in the *New York Times*. "The best and brightest at my agency and others dutifully exercise caution in substantive matters, avoid action and continually seek another clearance, another signature, another authorization until someone just finally says no."[17] This is not working with your compass; on the contrary, it is being worked by your compass. The passive voice captures it all; it represents process without purpose.

In response to such cynics, I would only ask, "Why bother?" Life is too short, work takes too much time and effort not to want to strive for excellence, not to want to leave a legacy of having made things better. We all need some purpose beyond simply serving and surviving. Process should never become an end in itself. Most decisions will have to be made under pressure of time, with incomplete information, no ideal choice, and uncertain effect. The good news is that few decisions are irrevocable; you can usually go back and fix things if they do not turn out as you hoped. What is important is that you be able to defend your decision on the evidence available at the time and that, if pressed, you can explain why other evidence was not available that might have led to a different choice.

Once you have made a decision, move on to the next problem. Do not agonize or dwell on it. Rethink a decision only after enough time has passed to allow for a constructive review or after new factors have surfaced that might affect the decision. Dean Acheson's description of Harry Truman's decisive style of operating is illuminating:

> His judgment developed with the exercise of it. At first it was inclined to be hasty as though pushed out by the pressure of responsibility, and—perhaps also—by concern that deliberateness might seem indecisiveness. But he learned fast and soon would ask, "How long have we got to work this out?" He would take what time was available for study and then decide. . . . No one can decide and act who is beset by second thoughts, self-doubt, and that most enfeebling of emotions, regret. With the President a decision was done with and he

went on to another. He learned from mistakes (though he seldom admitted them), and did not waste time bemoaning them.[18]

You cannot always expect to have the explicit authority to make a decision you consider necessary. If you wait for such clarity, you may find it never arrives. A good deal of governing in any institution takes place in a gray area of unclear mandates and overlapping jurisdictions, where an individual willing to assert authority may find he has more than he realized. Richard Armitage, a former Defense Department official, expresses this succinctly: "Always take 20 percent more authority than is granted. It's much better to have someone dial you back than to have to dial you forward." This involves some risk, although it can be minimized by letting your boss and others know what you are doing before or as you do it. Richard Perle, a former congressional aide and Defense Department official, urges people to take initiative in their jobs:

> The question always arises as to what authority you have. The answer is you have to assume you have absolute authority until somebody tells you otherwise, until somebody stops you. Because if you try to derive your authority, your freedom of action, from any other source, you are not going to have any fun, and you are not going to get much done. So I operated on the theory that it was within my authority to make decisions and do things and carry them out, right up until the moment that somebody was able to prove otherwise. And it's amazing how much you can get away with, how many people will acquiesce in that, if you seem determined and you seem to know what you are doing.

Never Forget Implementation

Although implementation is the work that follows a decision and translates intent into reality, it must be considered fully from the outset. Judgments about such matters as resources, organizational capacity, legal concerns, and politics must be considered as part of the decision itself. Implementation involves both technical support—the *ability* of people and organizations to carry out policy—and political support—the *willingness* to do the same. A popular case at Harvard's Kennedy School involved the Ford administration's ill-fated program to inoculate Americans against a feared epidemic of swine flu. Producing enough vaccine on time, finding the funds, arranging for the shots themselves, limiting liability—these and other "technical" issues all but doomed the effort.

Stanford University's provost Condoleezza Rice has it exactly right: "You don't have a policy unless you can get it done. You can have the best policy in the world on paper, it can be intellectually beautiful and elegant, but if you can't get it done, it never happened." My former Harvard colleague Steven Kelman makes a similar point:

> It simply will not do to say about a proposal, "It's a great idea, but it won't work." If there is no conceivable way to produce something successfully, it makes no more sense to talk about it as being a good idea "except for" the fact than it does to speak that way about an idea for a perpetual motion machine. If an idea won't work, it can't be great. Policy ideas must be crafted so they can be produced, and they must be changed if that is not feasible.[19]

Many people want to think that getting the desired decision is what really matters and that all else is secondary. Smart people are especially prone to falling into this trap, into believing that analyzing a situation and coming up with the right answer will persuade others to fall in line. But few issues are so clear that they do not admit various interpretations. Moreover, just because you or your agency has decided what needs to be done does not mean the rest of the world agrees. President Clinton learned this in spades in early 1993, when the successful launch of his economic program did not translate into accomplishment. As he put it later, "I think we had about a week's worth of strategy after February 17 to sell this and what we needed was about three months' worth of strategy."[20] David Stockman provides another example of the consequences of giving implementation short shrift. The time is January 1981, only days before Ronald Reagan entered the White House.

> Just before the inaugural, the president had approved, in principle, a series of symbolic "first day" directives designed to show that we would "hit the ground running" and come out slugging the federal monster. Among those were an across-the-board hiring freeze, a 15 percent cutback in agency travel budgets, a 5 percent cutback in consulting fees, and a freeze on buying any more furniture, office machines, and other such equipment. Within hours of the first full day I was swamped with urgent demands as to the meaning of these "directives." Did the travel cut apply to FBI agents on their way to apprehending a felon? Did the equipment freeze cover the blood-circulating machines essential to coronary bypass surgery? How did the hiring freeze impact the guy promised a federal job in Washington on February 1 who had already moved there from Utah? My staff and I held a desultory debate on it all and ended up exempting as much as we included.[21]

Often potential problems or resistance can be reduced or even eliminated by including in the decisionmaking process itself those most likely to be affected. Such a strategy can also improve both the quality of the decision and its prospects for implementation. A good example of this approach is the Clinton administration's National Performance Review—the effort to make government more efficient—which was conducted by the same officials who must implement any reform. This will surely ease implementation, just as the exclusion of members of Congress and their staffs from the process will complicate getting support for those measures Congress must approve.[22] Such inclusion may slow down the decisionmaking process, but the investment can pay off down the road, when implementation becomes paramount. The director of Mount Sinai Hospital, Barry Freedman, provides a textbook example of how implementation problems can upset good decisions:

We had a dedicated staff of IV [intravenous] nurses that we used to send to those patients requiring IV administration. What we discovered was in fact that when you have a centralized body doing that and going to the various patients, you spend an inordinate amount of time in transportation, in getting from one place to another. Why would we have only some 20 nurses doing this when we had 1,500 nurses trained as RNs, many with very advanced degrees? What we did not do was communicate it effectively. What we did not do was to enlist the participation of important constituency groups— physicians and the nurses . . . what we did not do was to build a broad enough consensus. We worked with a few physicians. We worked with 20 or 30 nurses. We worked with less than 20 physicians. And in an institution where you have 1,800 physicians, in an institution where you have 1,500 nurses, you need a broader base than that. . . . We had validated the approach, we had validated the concept, we certainly had the leadership of the respective entities informed and supportive, but we didn't get it to the troops.

Former governor Weld tells a similar tale about why presenting people with a fait accompli should be avoided:

On cutting the size of the government here and on our privatization efforts, it would have been handy if I'd gone to the public employee unions first and said, "Brothers and sisters, this is what we're doing, we have to do it, but let me assure you that not one tree is going to be cut down that is not absolutely necessary, or on privatization, that nobody is going to lose their job because of privatization, we'll find something somewhere else. . . ." These people were concerned about privatization's costing them jobs, and an inoculation would have been a good idea. And I just didn't know enough about government and government employees, about the sensitivities and nerve endings, when I came in. We just sort of plowed straight ahead.

Do Not Cut Corners

Keep your word and be straight with people. Effectiveness should not be confused with manipulation. The latter cannot be sustained, and your ability to have influence will atrophy over time if people suspect you of cutting corners, of cooking the books, of not presenting all the facts fairly, of not subjecting all proposals to equal rigor, of not including all those with a stake in a decision. You may get away with it once or twice, but before long your effectiveness will diminish. No one will trust you; no one will work with you. Your boss will discover you to be a liability. Worst of all, even your good ideas will suffer because they are associated with you.

At the Kennedy School, we used to talk a good deal about the concept of "thinking institutionally." Someone who thinks institutionally avoids cutting corners in order to prejudice the outcome of a certain decision or policy. This ethic is especially important in your relations with your east, with your colleagues. There may well be a short-term or immediate benefit, but you place your reputation and your future effectiveness in jeopardy. The blunt warning of Sheila Burke, chief of staff to Senator Robert Dole for more than a decade, is worth keeping in mind: "The first time you mislead someone is the last time you're effective. . . . Now, there are people who are obviously not very honest people, but that comes back to haunt them over time. People come to know that, they tend not to trust them, they won't develop relationships with them. They can do a job but I don't think they serve their bosses terribly well."

Do Your Homework

Master the material. You will tend to do well if you know the subject at hand better than anybody else. This means reading the memos, including any supporting materials and the fine print. It means staying abreast of developments in your field. Above all, it means subjecting your decisions to the most rigorous analysis available and making sure they stand up to the likely attacks or alternatives. If need be, set up an internal procedure along the lines of a "murder board" or mock trial that subjects your position or idea to criticism before you try it on the outside world. Lee Fischer, as attorney general of Ohio, subjected himself to multiple "moot courts" before he argued a case in court. Lawyers from his staff and from local firms and law schools were brought in to critique him. It can be embarrassing, even humiliating, but it is always better to make your mistakes when they do not count.

Avoid winging anything. If you know you have a weakness or a tendency to err in some area, make a special effort to examine it. "Check your blind spots" is good advice even if you are not behind the wheel. Richard Perle tells the following story about an experience he had while a young staffer to Senator Henry "Scoop" Jackson:

> I remember one occasion when the Egyptians began to deploy some missiles they'd received from the Soviets—they were called SCUDs—and we got word of this and Scoop decided to go up to the Senate press gallery . . . and Scoop said to me, "What is the range of the SCUD?" And I got it wrong. I said, "I think it's 420 miles." And Scoop went up to the press conference and announced that the Egyptians had started to deploy these weapons that had the range to reach Jerusalem and Tel Aviv, which of course was wrong. And within minutes after this was announced to the press gallery, it was being denied by the executive branch. I thought my young career was over, and it probably should have been, given a mistake of those proportions. . . . From that time on, I never to this day have been prepared to say something in public that I haven't checked and that I wasn't damn sure about. You can make mistakes about interpretations, but when it comes to facts you've just got to be right and you've got to be right every time—especially when you are putting the person you work for in an awkward position.

Control Your Schedule

A key to your success will be controlling your time and energy. There are only so many hours in the day and only so many calories in what you eat. There is a limit to how many things you can do—and an even greater limit to how many you can do well.

Controlling your time requires that you distinguish between the urgent and the important. Sometimes, during a genuine crisis for example, the two become one and the same; the 1990–91 crisis in the Persian Gulf was such a time for me. But these moments are rare. The danger comes when you allow the urgent (but not terribly important) to crowd out the truly important (but not terribly urgent).

Examples of what might fall into the category of "truly important but not terribly urgent" include planning, developing staff, and cultivating important colleagues and interest groups. A good way to test yourself is to compare your schedule with your agenda; if there is a large gap between the two, you are probably using your time poorly and are being driven by events. Stephen Covey put it succinctly in his popular book *The Seven Habits of Highly Effective People*: "The key is not to prioritize what's on your schedule, but to schedule your priorities."[23] James Strock, as the head of California's Environmental Protection Agency, had his own yardstick: "On questions of the use of my time, I try to think to myself, In thirty years, what's going to have made a difference? I try to think from ahead looking back."

This means treating long-term strategy as a necessity, not a luxury. Ellen Schall persuasively makes this point. "The demands of the immediate crises can easily drive out any long-term thinking or planning. Consequently, any public manager who wishes to succeed and to effect significant innovation must develop the capacity to build a long-term strategic agenda while simultaneously managing the short-term crises. Do not wait until the short-term crises are resolved. . . . A constant and unrelenting focus on the crises of the present will yield, at best, short-lived gains."[24]

Set Aside Time to Think

Some time every day or week ought to be left unscheduled so you can reflect on what you are doing and how you are doing it, what you are not attending to, and whether this is as it should be. During the Gulf crisis, I used to sit with my boss, Brent Scowcroft, several times a week just to think out loud about what it was we might be neglecting, what it was the other side might think of that we had not anticipated. So check that desk drawer of yours. Make sure that you have not lost sight of why you took the job. It is all too easy to get carried away and become the prisoner of your in-box or, worse, someone else's.

Sometimes it is necessary to monitor yourself to make sure you are getting it right. Listen to Antonia Bryson, at the time a deputy commissioner for air quality and programs in New York City's Department of Environmental Protection:

> What happens in government is that you always tend to get caught up in crises. . . . But it's helpful to sit back at the end of every week [and ask], Is this part of my long term plan of what I want to accomplish while I am in this job? . . . I do it a lot on the commute, or at the end of the day while I am home trying to unwind. I'll go over what happened during the day and I'll say, "It's been three or four weeks since I said I was going to do X in terms of moving my goal to revise this by six months from now, and my God, three weeks have gone by and I haven't done anything, so tomorrow I have to take this step in order to get that structure back in place or I have to call so and so to make sure we set up that meeting for this or whatever. . . . The higher up you get, the more you have to constantly examine how you are setting your own priorities. Are you going to the right meetings? Are you going to too many meetings? How can you use your staff members? Are you using them effectively to make sure that you yourself are spending your time on the right things and

accomplishing what you want to get accomplished? Am I spending my day efficiently? You definitely have to concentrate on that, because people are clamoring for your attention. . . .

Be Prepared to Work Hard

Working with all the points on your compass is tiring, even exhausting. I often thought that years in the government should be counted like those in the life of a dog, with one the equivalent of seven. The constant, often intense, interactions with others is a hallmark of life in the public sector and in large organizations. When it works, when you are able to persuade people and organizations to line up and work together, it is exhilarating. When you cannot, when ambition counteracts ambition to a degree even James Madison might not have wanted, it can be extremely discouraging. There is no substitute for resolve, for perseverance, for hanging in there.

Walter Plosila headed the Montgomery County [Maryland] High Technology Council, a nonprofit organization that works to bring together governments, industry, and higher education. He underscored the value of staying power:

> You have to be persistent. My grandparents came from Finland. We have a word in Finnish—*sisu*—which means be persistent and don't let somebody get the better of you. Stay in there and tough it out. Not be obstinate, but just continue to work at the problem and convince people and build support. Just because somebody said no initially doesn't mean that's the end of it and go do something else.

Do not expect it to be easy, either emotionally or psychologically. You will have days when you come to doubt yourself and wonder whether you are making a difference. The lack of a clear bottom line, the need to compromise and involve others—in short, all the traits that characterize the public sector—also have the effect of blurring accomplishment. Victories can be hard to come by; even completing a task sometimes can seem beyond reach. Typical in my experience are the questions raised by Mario Cuomo, who, in the early 1970s, was a young lawyer brought in to broker a compromise that would allow a controversial low-income housing project to move forward.

> That's what it's all about—it's climbing mountains without ever reaching the top, hoping, despite the slips and slides. That in the long run you're getting closer. And knowing, at least, that you're trying to get closer. It's the trying that counts. And the dull pain of frustration, the quick brief remorse over reversals, that's part of it. And so is the uncertainty—maybe that's the worst of all—not knowing whether you're really making progress, not knowing whether your judgment brought you closer or further from the top. Wondering whether you're right or wrong.[25]

You need to fight the doubts and be ready to persevere, to sell your policy retail, door to door, not showing your frustration or losing control. Kathleen Sheekey captures well this need to stay with something despite inevitable difficulties and the occasional defeat:

> In the course of a talk on lobbying, I said that I'd like my epitaph to read, "She made them squirm," because I think that a good lobbyist does make it at times uncomfortable for members of Congress not to do the right thing. Maggie Kuhn [the founder of the Grey Panthers] followed me and she said, "I like what you said Kathleen, but I'd like my epitaph to read, 'Here lies Maggie Kuhn under the only stone she left unturned.'"

Leave no stone unturned, then, but remember a complementary (and not contradictory) point: do not work harder than you need to. Save a gear for crises, for when it counts most. It is one thing to want to make a good impression and to try hard; it is another to be going at full speed when it is not necessary. It will only exhaust you and those around you, leaving you depleted for when something truly important comes along. Crises are inevitable, and, because of the stakes, they can have an impact that outweighs much of the normal work that came before. It makes sense to be at your best.

Do Not Make Enemies Carelessly

Not only do you spend most of your waking hours with your workmates, but your personality and your reputation for being decent can increase your effectiveness. Secretaries can help get your call returned or your meeting scheduled sooner than later. If there is a close judgment on some vote or decision, people may be affected by what they think of you. Also, you never know when it will be important to have someone well disposed toward you or when you will need a favor. Return phone calls, and, whenever possible, place them yourself. Unless you are quite senior and truly busy, few things are more pretentious than having your secretary place your calls for you. Politics and governing are tough enough without giving people an extra reason for opposing you and whatever it is you want to accomplish.

In short, never forget that policies do not make themselves—they are made by people. This is true at every point of the compass. When I asked George Bush what he thought was the key to effectiveness, he responded quickly: "Human relations." Why? "Because you get the most out of the people you are working with. If a respect level is there, or even a friendship level, they'll go the extra mile." Michael Dukakis, the former governor of Massachusetts (and the man who lost to Bush in 1988) makes a similar point: "All the cost-benefit analysis in the world isn't worth a plug nickel if you don't understand this: How you include and involve others in a system where either you act collectively or you go down the tubes."

Be Careful

Do not break the law. This applies to what you do on the job and what you do on your own time. Remember, there is no off duty and little privacy when you work in the public sector. Your life becomes something of a seamless web. This applies to personal behavior—getting drunk, using drugs, paying taxes, or arranging for child care—and also to matters involving conflicts of interest, be they financial or political, such as carrying out partisan political activity while in a public position. One lapse of judgment, one cut corner, can jeopardize everything that you have worked hard to achieve.

Nearly every outpost of government and of many other organizations has lawyers whose principal task is to tell you what you cannot do. While often a pain to listen to, such advice can be useful. A good rule of thumb is not to take advantage of your job—and the information to which it gives you access—for your benefit or the benefit of anyone you know. At a minimum, this means not investing in a company or any other endeavor that can be affected by anything you do or read about on the job. Your organization may also require that you declare what you invest in and then "recuse" (withdraw) yourself from matters that touch on these investments in any way. Such requirements can stay with you for years—for a statutory cooling-off period—or permanently; the bottom line is to avoid doing anything that is not easy to explain or that allows you to derive direct private benefit from public service.

But obeying the law is not enough. It may get you by the IRS—tax "avoidance" is acceptable, whereas tax "evasion" is not—but in public life, the equivalent of tax avoidance often fails to pass muster. It helps to ask yourself—preferably before you act—not simply whether what you are doing or are planning to do passes a legal test, but also whether it passes the smell test. Ask yourself how it would look, and how you would react, if it ended up in the newspaper the next day. This applies, in particular, to what you put down on paper or send via e-mail. If it does not feel right, if it could cause serious problems, forget it.

Maintain Perspective

It is possible that what you are doing is important in the larger scheme of things; alas, for most of us it probably is not.

Legendary college basketball coach Dean Smith captures this as well as anyone. "If you make every game a life-or-death proposition, you're going to have problems. For one thing, you'll be dead a lot."[26] Losing your sense of humor or ability to listen to what others are up to will not help. Do not take yourself any more seriously than necessary; a little bit of humility can go a long way. Do not forget, too, that you are you, not your job. Should you forget, you will be reminded when you are no longer in your position and the calls and invitations dry up.

Help maintain perspective by putting a limit on how much time you devote to work. You should be there as much as you need to be, but do not hang around for the sake of being seen. As the adage goes, it's not how many hours you put in, but what you put into the hours. You may impress some people with how hard and long you work—former budget director Richard Darman was reported to have left his coat on a chair near his office window to convey the impression he was working at all hours—but no amount of labor will compensate for the quality of your work.[27] Lawyers may bill for hours, but few people in the public sector get rewarded for effort alone. Instead, work only as long as you must, and make sure you set aside time for your personal life—for friends, for family, for health.

In the end, you will be no good to yourself or your boss if you allow your personal life to go to the dogs, for it will spill over and affect your performance. Few of us are indispensable. If you are run over one morning by a Greyhound bus and never make it to work, the office will go on without you—and only if the day is a slow one are some of your colleagues likely to manage to get to the hospital and visit you. Or, as they say in Rome, "*Morto un papa, se na fa un altro* (When a pope dies, they make another one)."[28]

Barbara Bush, the former first lady, expressed it well in her commencement talk to the women at Wellesley College in June 1990:

Cherish your human connections: your relationships with friends and family. . . . You are a human being first and those human connections—with spouses, with children, with friends—are the most important involvements you will ever make. At the end of your life, you will never regret not having passed one more test, not winning one more verdict, or not closing one more deal. You will regret the time not spent with a husband, a friend, a child, or a parent."

It is no less important to keep perspective of another sort. You can expect to come in for criticism, either by name or indirectly, when some enterprise you are associated with gets hammered by the press or by some interest group. It can get personal. It can get ugly. In my last job I was called a good many things not fit to appear in a family newspaper. I remember being attacked in one syndicated column as ill suited for my position overseeing Middle East policy because of my "close cultural ties to Israel"; ironically, I also received letters charging me with anti-Semitism and worse. Develop a thick skin, and get away from the office as often as need be to decompress.

Keep Lists

Lists are a key to effectiveness, more important than never giving anybody your only copy of anything or getting left behind by a motorcade. There is no better way to keep track of all that you need to do or check on. Do not trust your memory, no matter how good you think it is.

Conclusions

The political world is characterized—indeed defined by—a diffusion of power and authority; you can accomplish very little alone. Consequently, persuasion is the key to effectiveness. But you cannot persuade independent centers of power if you are not first in control of yourself. This is why the center of the compass is so important. You must determine what it is you want to accomplish and prepare yourself, and then proceed with discipline.

Focus is critical. You cannot accomplish all that you want, and certainly not all at once. The most effective people are those who choose goals that are limited in number, realistic for their position and circumstances, and true to what they believe in. Realizing these objectives requires discipline, defined here as a willingness to work hard and avoid distractions. This is easier said than done, and it is more likely to happen if you build into your life a regular examination of what you are doing and how you are using your time and other resources—and then compare your performance with your goals.

Effectiveness depends, too, on the close relationship between the center of the compass and the four points on the periphery. Determining your agenda requires a mixture of introspection and interaction, of asking questions of yourself and others, of speaking and listening. And always comparing the desirable and the possible. It is a constant theme of this book—namely, that the distinguishing characteristic of effective people is their ability to determine what they want to accomplish even as they demonstrate a willingness to work closely with others.

3

North:
Those for
Whom You
Work

No RELATIONSHIP IS MORE important than the one with your superiors, in part because they alone have the power to hire and fire. But the importance reflects something else: your relationship with your boss will be critical to your overall effectiveness. In many instances you will act indirectly through your North, while in other situations it is your perceived relationship with your boss that affects how other people and groups treat you. Except for the president or governor or mayor, almost everybody has a boss, so North is at the top of your compass for good reason.

Before Starting

The key to managing your relationship with those above you is studying their personalities and philosophies carefully. Research their past performance. Come to know their habits and operating styles. If you are to be effective, you must learn everything you can about them, and you must adjust to them. It can help you get a job; it can help you succeed.

By "studying" your boss, I do not necessarily mean looking up his or her entry in *Who's Who*. But by reading or talking with those who know him or her, you should learn what you can. You might find a connection that helps you form a bond. Or you may learn about some critical experience that will help you understand what makes him or her tick. You might simply learn about an issue or behavior to look out for or avoid.

Studying your boss begins with the initial interview. Learning about a potential boss before your first meeting can reduce the odds that you will not be prepared to discuss some issue. Think carefully, too, about what to ask and focus on. Do not try to nail down too much. Chemistry and general suitability count for more. But there are no guarantees in this world; no degree of access or influence, no role or mandate, can be granted for all time. Just about everything will depend on your performance, the performance of others, events, personality—and serendipity. The interview can help you get a sense of the lay of the land, a feel for what your boss will want from you, a rundown of your responsibilities, and a sense of your competition, but it probably cannot describe exactly what you will be doing and certainly cannot guarantee the extent of your authority.

So do not trouble yourself unduly with mandates and assurances that would count for little even if you received them. Job titles and position descriptions also tend to count for less and less over time. Good bosses learn to ignore the formal office diagrams of who is responsible for what and instead go to people who have shown they can produce the desired work in the time available. As any athlete knows, you play yourself either in or out of the starting lineup by your performance.

The rule, then, is that you should not expect or trust guarantees. But keep in mind two potential exceptions. The first concerns personnel. This can be critical if you are about to enter a mid-level or senior position and you need some ability to hire and fire (or transfer) people if you are to gain control of your new organization. A good example involves Robert S. McNamara, who in 1960 was President-Elect John F. Kennedy's choice for secretary of defense. Before agreeing to take the job, McNamara wrote a letter to Kennedy stating that he would come on two conditions: ". . . first, that he be left free to run the department as he thought best and to appoint whomever he wanted, and second, that he not have to go to parties or be a 'social secretary.'" There was even a line at the bottom where Kennedy was to sign. According to Robert Kennedy, the president-elect was impressed with McNamara's toughness but was "flabbergasted" at the letter and never signed it. Still, McNamara got the job and hired whom he wanted (unlike some of his cabinet colleagues). And, like it or not, he went to his share of parties.[1]

A second possible subject to discuss in advance is the question of whom you will be reporting through and to. If you have a legitimate concern that working for a certain individual will mean your views will not be heard by those to your far North, or your ability to deal effectively with your colleagues or outsiders will be compromised, consider pressing for a clear description of the reporting structure. But make sure you have a good case, because raising such concerns can appear petty. Moreover, such considerations should rarely be decisive; again, your performance will tend to determine your role more than any formal chain of command.

Exceptions do occur, though. Robert Strauss might have been one of the few people able to set the terms of his employment with a president and get away with it. He tells the following story about his conversation with Jimmy Carter when he was asked by the president to become the U.S. envoy to the Middle East:

[When I went to the Middle East], I said, "I can't report to [Secretary of State] Cy Vance. I'll report to you, Mr. President, and I know it will upset them in the State Department." He said, "How will we handle it?" I said, "Mr. President, that is your problem. You're the President, I'm not. I'll take the job and go over there and bust my ass for you. But I'm not going to report to the State Department. I don't fit in well there and I'm not going to be over there, surrounded by a bunch of assholes telling me what to do." I said to him, "I'm too old, I don't suffer fools patiently enough, and I'm too arrogant. And I don't have enough respect for the people I'd be working for. So it won't work." He said, "What is your idea?" I said, "Mr. President, if I will do it, I'll report to you and to the Secretary, but not through the secretary to you, that I'll promise you. And I'll take an office over in the Executive Office Building and build my own staff." And he said, "That's fine."

Strauss had a point, for in the Middle East, the fact that he was reporting to the president rather than some appointed official was likely to have a real impact on local leaders there, who look to the White House, not the State Department, as the true source of U.S. power and prestige. But if McNamara's attempt to clarify his relationship with the president was essentially harmless and Strauss's effort was justified, Alexander Haig's bid backfired. On Inauguration Day in January 1981, Haig, who was about to become secretary of state, handed the White House counselor Edwin Meese a twenty-page memorandum for the president's signature; it codified his and the State Department's primacy in overseeing all aspects of foreign policy. This was seen as a power play by other senior aides, and Haig's memorandum disappeared into the bottomless pit that was Meese's briefcase. What did not go away was the bad taste in people's mouths that told them that Haig was not a team player.[2] A year and a half later, Haig was history.

Adapting to Your Boss

Studying your boss becomes especially important once you have accepted a position and started work. Everyone has a particular way of doing business. Some people, for example, like to consider an issue by reading about it. Others prefer to hear positions argued out in their presence. Needless to say, you would be wise to prepare memos for the former and rehearse your debating skills for the latter.

Sir Charles Powell, for seven years a close advisor to British prime minister Margaret Thatcher, makes clear the importance of understanding your boss's operating style—for both your effectiveness and your boss's:

> What she really enjoyed was argument. She tested views out in argument. She sometimes took outrageous positions simply just to see what you would suggest. But if at the end of the discussion she thought your view was better than hers, she would shamelessly adopt your view, without of course ever admitting that she had changed her mind at all. It was a seamless transition. Therefore, it wasn't nearly as difficult as people think, provided they were prepared to argue with her. Arguing with her was quite a fiercesome business, because it was no holds barred. One of our ministers was very frightened about dealing with her, and therefore tended to succumb meekly, which was a mistake, because it meant sometimes that without opposition she did some fairly stupid things.

Dick Morris, a close advisor to President Bill Clinton until scandal forced him to resign, recounts an episode that demonstrates how a failure to understand your boss can be bad for both the advisor and the person in charge.

> At an Oval Office meeting about the '96 campaign, [Don] Baer presented a concise, well-structured, and effective draft stump speech to the President. Clinton read through it and then talked about all the other things he was thinking of that day that might go into the speech. I was about to say that his stump speeches lacked discipline and that he should focus on the speech text Baer had given him. Instead, Baer jumped in, trying to please the President, and instead of defending the excellent speech he'd just presented, offered to include

all of Clinton's meandering thoughts in a revised version. I
watched the President's face as Baer spoke. It reflected the
feeling that Don had caved in too easily, that he should have
stood his ground. Clinton wants to be challenged. Subordinates who give way unnerve him.[3]

Some bosses are all business. Small talk bores them. Meetings
that take more than fifteen minutes leave them restless. Others
prefer bull sessions. Some are morning people; others are bears
before a few cups of coffee. In each case, you have to tailor yourself to what works. Early in his career, George Shultz worked for
Arthur Burns, who was the chairman of the president's Council of
Economic Advisors. According to Shultz, "Arthur liked to talk and
stayed late around the office. So whenever I prepared a memorandum for him, I would bring it up to his secretary around four
o'clock in the afternoon, hoping that he would look at it about
4:30 or 5:00 and ask me to discuss it with him. He often did, providing me the opportunity to sit and talk, sometimes for lengthy
periods of time. This was a great education."[4] And a great way to
build a relationship with one's boss.

David Stockman, Reagan's first budget director, recounts a tale
about being on the losing side of a debate—in large part because
one of his colleagues (or competitors) had out-studied their common boss before a very important meeting. In 1981, when the first
real administration budget debates were being waged, Stockman
found himself arguing with Defense Secretary Caspar Weinberger
and others over how much the defense budget ought to be
increased. The outgoing Carter administration had increased
defense spending substantially; the question was how much more
the Reagan administration would increase that already higher
amount.

The issue came to a head in early September, when Reagan
met with the principal protagonists. Weinberger went first, taking his allotted fifteen minutes and turning them into an hour.
The coup de grâce came at the end. Weinberger's last chart
depicted three soldiers: one, a pygmy carrying no rifle (the

Carter budget); the second a "wimp who looked like Woody Allen, carrying a tiny rifle" (the Stockman proposal); and the third, "G.I Joe himself, 190 pounds of fighting man, all decked out in helmet and flak jacket and pointing an M-60 machine gun. . . ."[5] Taking the floor, Stockman argued that a smaller increase represented the more responsible fiscal path while still improving defense capability markedly. Stockman may have won the argument on the merits, but Weinberger (supported by Secretary of State Alexander Haig) carried the day. He had simply taken into account what was most likely to work with Reagan. Stockman would have been wise to highlight the considerable overlap between the competing proposals, as well as how much money this would free up to buy other things close to Reagan's heart. More important, Stockman should have gone to greater lengths to enlist allies from the executive branch and Congress known to be worried about the economic consequences of Weinberger's plan. Even these tactics may have failed to persuade Reagan, but his by-the-numbers approach to the issue all but ensured that Stockman never really had a chance.

Access to your boss is important. Try to get as much as you need but do not waste it, or you will find yourself getting less than you need. You should learn quickly how much appetite your boss has for detail, how much information he or she desires before authorizing you to take action. But do not abuse your access by "hanging around" and becoming a nuisance—or by offering advice on subjects that are outside your purview and on which your boss looks to others. As Robert Strauss likes to say, "Advice that isn't sought has very little value."

Timing is important too. Cultivating those close to your boss— whether they are close in the physical sense, such as his secretary, or those who are close personally—can be invaluable. Like most people, your boss has moods and is affected by events at home or at work that you will know nothing about. A good idea can be shot down for no other reason than you brought it up at the wrong time. Before going over to see Brent Scowcroft in his office, I often phoned his secretary, Florence Gantt, to learn how much pressure he was under at that moment and how much time he had. Depending on her response, I could reduce the scope of my agenda or even ask that the meeting be postponed if it had been set up at my request.

It is important to keep in mind that no two bosses are the same; what worked well with one might not work at all with another. An old college friend of mine, Kenneth Kay, learned this lesson when he went to work for Senator Max Baucus of Montana after years of being an aide to Congressman (later Mayor) Ed Koch of New York:

> Ed Koch had an opinion on everything. Absolutely everything. I'll never forget the first week I was in Baucus's office. I was asked to do a letter, a constituent letter. And so I used the Koch formula to write a Baucus letter. And so it goes, "Thank you so much for writing on this subject. Unfortunately, we don't agree on this matter. Perhaps we'll agree on another one. I'm enclosing a statement on both the matter you disagree with and one maybe we agree on." That's how Ed would do it. Max comes into the office yelling, "What the hell is this?" I said, "This is how I answer constituent mail." He goes, "We don't answer Montana mail this way. We don't tell somebody we disagree with them."

What might Kay have done to save himself that exchange? He could have perused the office files to get a sense of the writing style of his new boss and then adopted it. Or, if he disagreed, Kay might have raised (either in a memorandum or in conversation) the possibility of the office's moving to a more direct approach in its responses to constituents. The lesson is clear, however: study your boss carefully and adapt when possible to his or her style.

Two points require clarification. First, adjusting to your boss does *not* mean always taking your cue from him. You can and should lead from below. You can provide suggestions, ideas, proposals; you can (and sometimes should) take risks. Being a subordinate does not mean being reactive or passive.

Second, adjusting your behavior to fit the style and preferences of your superior does *not* mean you should fashion or slant your arguments to fit his preferences or biases. Tailoring your arguments should not be confused with trimming your sails. "Yes men" (or women) are neither valued nor respected; for good reason does Machiavelli advise his prince to shun sycophants. Moreover, you are not being helpful or loyal to your boss by holding back. A chief ingredient of loyalty is telling your boss what you think is right and best. You owe only your best judgment, counsel, advice. Your boss may choose not to accept it, but it is your obligation to give it.

Showing Loyalty Up

Speaking candidly can cause disagreements and even arguments. So be it. I am not encouraging shouting matches with your boss—although, again, the style of your presentation and conversation will vary, depending on your boss's personality and your relationship. But you do not serve him well if you fail to note a flaw in what is being proposed. Better to avoid a mistake than to clean up after one. If you doubt this, just ask those people around Ronald Reagan who had doubts about the impact of his policies on the budget deficit and never spoke up. Or those at NASA who wished they had done more to prevent the launching of the space shuttle *Challenger* on that cold January morning.

Dean Acheson had the sort of relationship with Harry Truman that could serve as a model for everyone:

> It is important that the relations between the President and the Secretary of State be quite frank, sometimes to the point of being blunt. And you just have to be deferential. He is the President of the United States, and you don't say rude things to him—you say blunt things to him. Sometimes he doesn't like it. That's natural, but he comes back, and you

argue the thing out. But that's your duty. You don't tell him only what he wants to hear. That would be bad for him and everyone else.[6]

Elizabeth Reveal has this to say on the subject:

You don't serve a chief elected official well if you are not prepared to tell him what you think. As far as I am concerned, that's the only thing that people ever bought of mine is my judgment. Sometimes it is right, and sometimes it's wrong. But if I am not offering it candidly, if I am doing *any* kind of dissembling or telling them what I think they want to hear, then I don't think I am serving them at all. And in my experience that approach has made me much closer to chief elective officials than my peers, because so few people treat them that way and they need it and they respect it and they like it. So that's the most important thing to me, telling them what they *need* to hear, not what they *want* to hear.

Again, Robert Strauss had to deal with this issue as well when he was asked to discuss a sensitive personnel matter with President Reagan. Knowing that his advice would not be well received, Strauss in effect warned Reagan with the tale of his first visit to the Oval Office.

I said, "Mr. President, I've been up here with other presidents before you. The first one who ever had me up here was Lyndon Johnson. And he asked me what I thought about Vietnam, and I told him every single thing that I thought he wanted to hear. Not one single word of which I believed. I just lied. He intimidated me and I couldn't tell him the truth. And I left there and I felt like a common prostitute, so dirty." And I said to President Reagan that night, "Mr. President, I made up my mind that if any President was ever foolish enough to ask my advice again, I'd try to make up for that." And since then I have never lied to the President or misled him because of his office.

As it turned out, Reagan appreciated what Strauss told him—even if he didn't like it. But speaking up is easier said than done. Joseph Heller, in his wonderfully cynical novel *Good as Gold*, describes a meeting between Ralph, a presidential aide, and Bruce Gold, a would-be assistant. Gold speaks first.

> "What would I have to do?"
>
> "Anything you want, as long as it's everything we tell you to say and do in support of our policies, whether you agree with them or not. You'll have complete freedom."
>
> Gold was confused. He said delicately, "I can't be bought, Ralph."
>
> "We wouldn't want you if you could be, Bruce," Ralph responded. "This President doesn't want yes-men. What we want are independent men of integrity who will agree with all our decisions after we make them. You'll be entirely on your own."
>
> "I think I might fit in," Gold decided.[7]

Some people accused General Colin Powell, the chairman of the Joint Chiefs of Staff, of disloyalty for opposing President Clinton's aim of opening up the armed forces to gay men and women. Powell forcefully presented his view that it would not be in the nation's interest to proceed as his boss desired. This was proper. Imagine if he had kept his objections to himself; Clinton could have gone ahead, thinking the reform would pass muster with the military, only to initiate a major fight that could have dominated the first months of his presidency and perhaps impeded the very change he sought. Powell did him a favor by registering his opposition and by slowing the pace of reform to a speed the system was prepared to tolerate.

You do yourself no favor either by pulling your punches. Do it even once and you will forever create doubts about your intellectual honesty. Robert Reischauer, a colleague of mine at the Brookings Institution who once headed the Congressional Budget Office (CBO), made the case for telling it like it is in a statement to his former colleagues. "CBO is of no use at all unless we shoot straight. If we deviate one little bit because of politics or pressure, everything we do becomes suspect because virtually everything we do is controversial."[8]

You have the added obligation to give your advice in private. Your boss should never read about your opposition in the newspaper or hear about it in the cafeteria from someone else. There is no quicker way to undermine trust and discourage open discussion than to go public or to outside channels with your dissent. All you will guarantee is that your advice will no longer be sought and that you will not be included in the decisionmaking circle the next time around.

You should also avoid surprising your boss or allowing him or her to be surprised by others, especially if the news is bad. Robert White, when he was chief of staff to California governor Pete Wilson, made a point of raising this concern in his conversation with new employees. After telling them never to forget that they are always representing the governor, he added, "Always tell me the truth, and if there is bad news, goddamn it, don't hide it from me. And if there's a problem coming down the line, it is your job to be able to go out and anticipate that problem and be able to have recommendations along the way as it comes along. Don't wait till the last minute." Bad news rarely improves with age; it is almost always better to get it out and begin dealing with it rather than putting it off.

Retired Admiral William Crowe, also a former chairman of the Joint Chiefs of Staff, tells a useful story about the importance of candor. Crowe disagreed with the proposal to ban all ballistic missiles that President Reagan made when he met with President Gorbachev at the Reykjavik (Iceland) Summit in October 1986. Afterward, knowing he would be asked for his views by Congress, Crowe found an opportunity at a meeting of senior national security aides to let Reagan know of his opposition. It was too late to change the policy, and it meant risking his relationship with his boss by letting him know he disagreed, but Crowe decided it was wiser than having Reagan learn of his dissent by seeing him on television. The president was not bothered by Crowe's view, and neither the policy nor Crowe's relationship with his boss changed as a result.[9]

Equally important is faithful implementation of a decision once it is made. Nothing is worse than the individual who undermines a decision if it does not go his or her way—except perhaps for the individual who never spoke up when the chance arose to influence matters. A boss has the right to expect discipline—defined here as supporting a decision even if you argued against it. James Baker, the former secretary of state, is clear on the importance of this trait: "My idea of 'good' is somebody who is willing to give you his best, come up with the idea and surface it to you, and that you can count on as loyal. When I say 'loyal' what I really mean is that if they get overruled on a policy approach they are not going to go trashing the operation to the press. That's the real test of loyalty."

This, then, is what "loyalty up" is all about. You owe it to your superior to give him or her your best advice in private and then go along and implement the decision faithfully regardless of whether it was your own preferred course as well. General Colin Powell is persuasive on this point:

> If you are part of the decision process, you have been brought in and your views have been heard, the issue has been fully vetted, and then your leader makes a decision, you've got no bitch. You can't go out and undercut that decision—not and serve honorably. . . . I say what's on my mind and give my best advice and I don't particularly care whether it is favorably received or not. It's not a measure as to whether the advice is favorably received. The measure is, was it delivered? I have never had a situation with a President where they will ever be able to turn around and say, Why didn't you tell me? They hear the good, the bad. But I don't ever want to have some President all wrapped around his underwear in some awful situation, à la Kennedy in the Bay of Pigs, and nobody told him. My greatest responsibility is to provide advice to the President whether the advice is consistent with his own views

at that time. . . . Advice doesn't have to be accepted, it just has to be listened to.

You also need to consider when and how often to go all out—"go to the mat"—to win a debate with your boss. You do not want to do it too often and get a reputation for being the resident gadfly, which is what happened in the 1960s with Chester Bowles and his successor, George Ball. Both served as the number two person in the State Department, both became regular critics of the U.S. policy in Vietnam, and both suffered for it. You risk being shut out or, even if not, you may be heard but not listened to. Choose your subjects and your moments alike.

You also need to choose the style of your approach. Prolonging a debate tends to become counterproductive once you have exhausted your arguments. Repetition and shouting only make matters worse. Style can be particularly important for careerists who disagree with elected officials or political appointees. Sometimes indirect can be best. Fred Smith, a respected career official who runs an office in the Pentagon, offers this advice to the civil servant confronted by what he or she thinks are misguided suggestions from his political superior:

> You don't tell them it's cockamamie; that's what some of my guys try to do and I have to walk them back. You try to nibble at the edges. You try to write the paper, you try to present the facts and back up your position. You try to walk it back slowly toward the direction you want, but you don't tell them this is all miscast and dumb and ridiculous, because then they're just going to dig in their heels and they're going to tell you that they're now in charge.

Working Successfully with Your Boss

Your relationship with your boss can and should change. Trust and confidence grow with time and experience and proven performance. There tends to be less need to ask for authority to do something or make some decision, in part because you have a better idea of what is wanted. Early in your or your boss's tenure, though, you should be careful of exercising too much authority. Time normally makes it safer to act without first checking; if you happen to be wrong, you will probably have some capital in your account that can be drawn on.

I enjoyed a good relationship with my boss Brent Scowcroft—but only after a shaky start. First, on a trip to the Middle East, I was off consulting with Israeli, Palestinian, and Arab officials about the future of the peace process without (in his view) keeping him sufficiently informed. Suddenly a cable—more a rocket—arrived, making it clear he did not share my assessment of the situation (not to mention my assessment of myself and what I was doing). Then, a few weeks later, I got blasted a second time, in this case for signing off on a public statement that Scowcroft disagreed with after he read about it in the newspapers. The moral of this tale should be clear: begin carefully and expand your autonomy only gradually, after you are confident that you have a reasonable feel for your boss's thinking and after he has developed some confidence in yours. You never want to get too far out in front of your boss, especially not at the beginning.

Another part of studying your boss is assessing his or her strengths and weaknesses and considering how best to maximize your own usefulness. If your boss is a big-picture person, then you have the responsibility (and the opportunity) to make sure all the details fit. If your boss is an expert on one part of his or her turf but is relatively weak on another, it makes sense for you to concentrate when possible on the area of weakness. Similarly, if you are relatively strong in one area, by all means play to your strength if it will serve your boss and your organization.

As a rule, you should know more detail about a given issue in your domain than your superior. It was my responsibility, not Scowcroft's, to stay abreast of every twist and turn of the Middle East peace process. Organizations are like inverted pyramids: the higher one goes, the more one exchanges depth for breadth. What you spend 50 percent of your time on may represent just

5 percent of what your boss worries about. You have the obligation to be on top of things—and your boss is right to expect it.

You also need to deliver what you promise or are assigned to do. Take deadlines seriously; do your best to meet every one. I used to tell my students that people either got it done or had an excuse. Some excuses are truly creative, and some stories about children, dogs, and computers are no doubt even true. But few stories, no matter how interesting, constitute an acceptable substitute for getting the job done on time. Make it easier on yourself by building in some time for Murphy's Law to operate without undermining you. Have a fallback. If you sense you are not going to meet a deadline, the sooner you say so, the better. There may still be time to adjust expectations and schedules. But a last-minute screw-up is sure to bring out the worst in everyone.

Beware of not being straight with your boss about what you do and do not know. The three most useful words in your relationship might well be, "I don't know." It helps if they are not uttered too often; whenever they are, follow up quickly with, "But I will get back to you soon with the answer." Of course, ignorance can be humiliating. When I was a young State Department official, I once used all my bureaucratic skills to get inside a meeting at the White House between President Reagan and Prime Minister Özal of Turkey. As it progressed, a complicated question arose concerning U.S.–Turkish trade. Suddenly, my boss (George Shultz) and James Baker (then White House chief of staff) turned to me for an explanation. After I filibustered on for about twenty seconds, Baker cut me off with a blistering, "So you don't know the answer either." Shultz laughed; I nearly died. Never again have I tried to fake it.

Know when to complain. You should not do it often, however, because for the most part your job is to lighten the load on your boss, not make it worse. Also, avoid complaining that you were cut out of a debate (or not invited to a meeting or given a chance to weigh in on some matter) when in fact you had nothing to add. You do not want to go to the mat on procedure; save it for when you can clearly demonstrate how much better a decision would have resulted if you had been included in the process.

One last point on reading your boss. You can spare yourself a good deal of frustration and discomfort if you come to understand his or her management style. It makes no sense to wish for frequent praise or to assume that you are doing something wrong if you work for someone who is spare with feedback or "attaboys." At the same time, a lack of criticism might mean you are doing poorly if you work for a person who tends to lower the boom with little warning. Do not expect your boss to communicate his feelings directly or clearly; it is up to you to make sure of your status, by asking either your boss or someone who is in a position to know.

Making Your Case: Writing the Persuasive Memo

A crucial dimension of your relationship with your boss is your ability to persuade him to choose a preferred course of action or to take your side in an important debate. Sometimes you will be able to make your case in person; on other occasions it will be on paper, in a memorandum. Either way, you must make it effectively.

Odds are that you will most often present your arguments on paper, which uses your boss's time more efficiently: a memo can be read whenever convenient, and it can travel places more easily than you can. For relatively junior people in an organization, memos have the potential to give their ideas a degree of access to high-level people that they themselves might not experience for years.

Writing effective memos is an art, and you should keep in mind the following guidelines:

Memos should be as short as possible. There is always an enormous amount to read and do, and time is a scarce commodity. Do not waste your boss's time by writing any more than is necessary; do not waste your own for the same reason. Put supporting documentation and materials in an addendum or tab if you must include them at all. Practice what Strunk and White preach in their classic essay, *The Elements of Style*: "Vigorous writing is concise. A sentence should contain no unnecessary words, a paragraph no unnecessary sentences, for the same reason that a drawing should have no unnecessary lines and a machine no unnecessary parts. This requires not that the writer make all his sentences short, or that he avoid all detail and treat his subjects only in outline, but that every word tell."[10]

The purpose of a memo should be clear from the outset. Are you raising a question or asking for a decision? Are you preparing your boss for a meeting or some other event? Are you providing a "think piece" meant to stimulate or provoke or inform? If there is a specific hook—be it a meeting, a trip, a vote, or an action that is required—say so.

Anticipate what issues are of concern to your boss. Your memo is more likely to be read and remembered if it addresses something of genuine concern to your boss, not just you. Avoid wasting time—yours as well as your boss's—with issues that are frivolous or that you can decide on your own. If your subject is not on your boss's mind when you start out, make the case early why it ought to be.

Figure out how much work a memo needs to accomplish. Will you have a chance to follow it up with a conversation or a meeting? Will there be a chance to do more? Or is this memo your only shot? Do no more or less than is necessary.

A memo is not an Agatha Christie novel. Do not save your punch line for the last paragraph. Take a lesson from journalists and get what matters most to you (and the reader) in the lead paragraph. You can always explain how it is you arrived at your position in the body of the memo.

The analysis must be rigorous. Your argument should not be shaped by your own conclusion or recommendation. Indeed, even those who reach a different conclusion should be able accept your analysis. Do not cook the books to make your point. If you have to, it is probably a good idea to rethink your own position.[11]

The real costs and benefits of each option should be assessed over a period of time that is relevant. For example, it is not intellectually honest to compare startup costs with immediate returns if over the life of the project the costs and benefits evolve significantly, as is often the case. In addition, when making cost projections, include the error or degree of uncertainty in your assessment. Do not be afraid to include soft, intangible factors that may not be easily measured but can still affect the decision at hand; sometimes they are the most important. Also, if by choosing one option you forfeit the chance to do something else, say so; opportunity cost should be an important factor in any assessment.

One of your options should be the status quo. Like the other options, this one should be assessed fully. At a minimum, it offers a base-line. And sometimes patience and "staying the course" promise to yield the best result. "Don't just do something, stand there" can be good advice.

Divorce politics and partisanship from analysis. Depending on a host of factors, ranging from the question at hand to your rela-tionship with the intended recipient of the memo, it may be appropriate to include political (partisan) considerations. If you do include them, they should be kept distinct from the rest of your analysis. Better yet, save any political comments for when you see your boss informally. Nothing is more likely to leak and create a sensation than political judgments taken out of context.

If there is relevant history, include it. If a course of action similar to what you are proposing or assessing has been tried, say so, and say what was learned. A historic parallel can have a powerful effect on the reader. Just be sure that it is relevant and not overdrawn. Assess what resembles the past and what is different.[12] Every impropriety is not Watergate, every failure is not the Bay of Pigs. Do not reach for your umbrella and shout "Munich" unless you really think it is a case of appeasement that will have large-scale, adverse consequences.

Include what will be necessary to implement your recommendation. The best idea in the world is wasted if you cannot figure how to get it done. You are obligated to show how anything you propose can be accomplished and financed.

Make sure that you include any weaknesses or risks in your own case. This comes under the heading of not surprising the boss. Also, it is always best to provide full disclosure; you can then go on to explain why the obstacles do not sink your argument.

Overcome an opposing argument or perspective by preempting it. Show why another position is deficient in a rigorous and honest way. Take on your opponents, but on your own turf. Do not leave it to them to present their own case without subjecting it to the scrutiny you can bring to bear.

Do not provide analysis without offering your judgment about what is the best option. Senator Daniel Patrick Moynihan, who was a senior domestic policy official in the Nixon administration, puts it this way: "Men who counsel caution in a President do him no disservice, but they do not add much to his day."[13] Similarly, criticism alone rarely satisfies if your boss has to do something. He needs your thinking on the best available option, no matter how bad it might be, even if it means doing nothing. Walter Isaacson highlighted this in his biography of Henry Kissinger. "One lesson he learned was that a President does not need a lot of people who tell him what he cannot do; it is better to be one of those telling him what he *can* do, or at least offering preferable alternatives."[14]

Condoleezza Rice makes a similar point:

> Never just say "I disagree," but have an answer for what an alternative might be. In academia, I love intellectual back-and-forths, just sitting down and hammering it out and coming together to some consensus. You do some of that in government. But mostly you don't have time. It's very important that you think through—before you go in—what you believe an alternative might be, and so you say, "I disagree with that, but here's a better way that we could go."

Make sure the options are real ones. The classic cold war memo, one that lays out the three options of launching an all-out nuclear attack, surrendering, or some wise, preferred middle course, does the reader no good. The first two options are so flawed, they are useless; the middle option is so big that it hides the real choices. It is far better to rule out the nonstarters and present the real choices, their consequences, and what they would require to implement.

Be sure of your facts. As the saying goes, you're entitled to your own opinion, but not to your own set of facts. There is no faster way to discredit your work than to get something specific wrong. Never confuse a fact with an assumption or a prediction, no matter how confident you may be.

Be explicit and careful about your assumptions and your methodology. As with facts, you do not want your ideas or proposals to be discredited because of some minor flaws you introduced as you built your argument.

Be aware of appearances. Typos matter. It is difficult not to associate sloppiness in form with sloppiness in content.

Memos can take on a life of their own. You cannot be sure who will read your memo. Early in his tenure, Secretary of Defense Les Aspin was hurt by a memo several of his staffers left in the G: drive of their computer. The memo suggested that he should only go through the motions of consulting with the military leadership on the question of modifying the status of homosexuals in the armed forces. Needless to say, the military leaders were not amused to learn that what they thought was an opportunity to affect policy was little more than a sham. Before you send a memo, always ask yourself how it might look in the newspaper or help someone with a different agenda.

When to Leave

One question remains about your relationship with your North: when to tell your boss that you are leaving. There are all sorts of reasons, some of them good ones, for leaving a job. They can be personal—a desire to spend more time with family and friends, a desire to make more money, a desire for greater challenge or growth, physical health. What distinguishes all these decisions is not that they are voluntary, although they are, but rather that they represent a choice to move on to something else, be it another position or way of life or whatever.

I say this to distinguish between leaving on your own terms and quitting. Quitting (or "resigning," if you prefer) a job is not so much a move *to* anywhere as a move *away* from where you are. One should only quit for reasons of principle. If you are committed strongly to a certain policy, or oppose one with great intensity, and the decision goes against you, it may be time to consider resigning. I do not subscribe to the peculiarly British notion of resigning when something turns out badly on your watch, as happened when Foreign Secretary Lord Carrington left over his failure to anticipate and head off Argentina's invasion of the Falkland Islands. Carrington was no more responsible than countless others, and by resigning he deprived his government of his valuable counsel at a crucial time. There is such a thing as being too responsible. Attorney General Janet Reno ignored calls that she resign in the wake of the April 1993 tragedy in Waco, Texas, in which more than eighty members of a religious cult perished. Just because a decision proves wrong or a policy fails, one should not conclude there were better options given what was known and advised at the time.[15]

The test comes if you cannot accept and implement the decision as if it were your own. Then it is time to move on. This situation does not arise with great frequency. Almost every day small decisions are made, and some of these will not be to your liking; as the old line goes, you win some and you lose some. Do not let these daily skirmishes get under your skin. Avoid any serious thought of quitting unless the issue at hand raises matters of high policy and principle.

As a yardstick, keep in mind the example of former secretary of state Cyrus Vance, who resigned after the failed attempt to rescue the American hostages held in Iran in 1980. Vance opposed the operation and told President Carter that he would resign in its aftermath if the decision were made to go ahead—regardless of the results.[16]

You may also have grounds for resigning if you feel increasingly uncomfortable with a pattern of decisions. It may not be any single decision that puts you over the top but, rather, a series of choices that demonstrate that you are not having much effect and that the policies advocated by those to your North are hardly ever ones you can endorse. (This was apparently what led William S. Ritter Jr. to resign publicly in August 1998 from the U.N. Special Commission—the organization created to monitor Iraqi weapons of mass destruction.)[17] Whether to resign in such circumstances is a tough call; ask yourself whether you are having any impact that might justify your staying or whether you might benefit in other ways by remaining, even if having influence is not one of them. And never forget the "compared with what" calculation. It is rarely wise to leave a job without having a good idea about what to do next.

These complicated issues are vividly illustrated by George Kenney's resignation from the State Department in 1992. Kenney, the son of a career foreign service officer, was the number-two man on the two-person Yugoslav desk at the time, and he had grown increasingly unhappy with the U.S. policy of remaining at a safe distance from events in the former Yugoslav republic of Bosnia-Herzegovina. Kenney's account of his experience shows just how difficult a decision to quit can be:

> I had to decide whether quitting would matter. Doing the [press] guidance all the time, and seeing how we reacted to it, I figured that if I could publicly embarrass the administration—say, well gosh, you're not doing this and you're not doing this, even though you say you are doing something— that they would have to react and in reacting perhaps do something constructive. Secondly, my conscience bothered me. I felt I was doing a really good job at producing material that the system wanted and that somehow I was contributing to making things worse. So I just didn't want to be a part of it. . . . I talked it over with some of my colleagues, with my

family and friends. Basically, everybody told me not to do it because there I was, a mid-level officer, and they said, "Nobody is going to listen to you. You're going to sink like a stone without making a ripple. So why do it? Just put up with the stuff and then go on and do something else." My father is telling me not to do it. He's saying, "You're doing well in the service, just wait. In ten years you are going to be in a policy-making position, and you've had a rapid rise, so why mess it up?" I said, "Well, I think people are going to listen to me and I think it's more important than me."

Kenney's decision, although widely reported in the media, had no discernible effect on U.S. policy; that said, it may have allowed him to sleep better, no small consideration. Nevertheless, it is probably not a good ideas to quit more than once or twice in a career. Not only do you want to avoid getting a reputation as a quitter, but a history of resigning suggests a degree of emotional volatility that scares people off. Even if you convince prospective employers that your decisions to quit were justified, they may conclude that you are not dependable. Still, keep in mind the advice of George Shultz: "You can't do a job well if you want it too much. You have to be willing to say goodbye."[18]

You also need to be careful about threatening to resign as a technique to get your way. As Alexander Haig learned to his regret, your offer may be accepted when you least expect—or want—it.[19] If you have the leverage, however, a threat to resign can be a powerful negotiating gambit. George Shultz used it to good effect in late 1985 when, by threatening to resign, he stopped the Reagan administration's plan to administer polygraph (lie detector) tests on a widespread basis.

Just as important as the decision about whether to quit is how you go about it. As a general rule, it is best to go gently into the night. To go noisily and in effect turn on your former colleagues will prompt any prospective employer to wonder whether you might do the same thing the next time. To resign quietly and with dignity can enhance your value as someone of principle and character.

Conclusions

If persuasion is the key to effectiveness, then persuading your bosses, or those to your North, is a critical part of any job. Indeed, as will become evident, the ability to persuade your boss has an added dividend: not only will it make you more influential with him or her, but it will make you more influential with your staff, your colleagues, and with others, for they will come to realize that your thinking has the potential to become your boss's thinking.

Study your boss well; it will pay off. But never forget that adapting your approach to maximize your effectiveness is not to be confused with adopting positions because you believe they are held or sought. Always make good use of your time and your boss's, and you are likely to increase your access. Remember, too, that meetings and memos should always have a purpose: before getting started, determine the desired outcome and focus all your energy on how to influence your boss's thinking or get the guidance you need.

In the end, you make yourself look good by making your boss look good. He or she may be willing to assist you in the future. You increase the odds of this happening by showing loyalty in all its dimensions—especially by demonstrating intellectual honesty. Again, North is the most important direction you face; cultivating it should be a high priority.

4

South:
Those
Who Work
for You

IF NORTH REPRESENTS YOUR MOST important set of relationships, South represents your most important set of decisions. You cannot usually choose your boss (other than by deciding whether to take or stay in a job), but you can have some choice over who works for you, how you organize them, how you motivate them, and, above all, how you use them.

Leading vs. Managing

A great deal has been written on the subject of leadership—what it is and how to do it. John Gardiner, the founder of Common Cause, offers a formal definition: "Leadership is the process of persuasion or example by which an individual (or leadership team) induces a group to pursue objectives held by the leader or shared by the leader and his or her followers."[1] He goes on to list no fewer than fourteen attributes of leaders, ranging from stamina and intelligence to qualities of character and interpersonal skills. Another book on leadership puts it this way: "The essence of leadership is very simple. It is to motivate people to perform to their maximum potential to achieve goals or objectives that you set."[2]

A good many people who have written about leadership and management draw a sharp distinction between the two. The following is typical: "Management is the bottom line focus: How can I best accomplish certain things? Leadership deals with the top line: What are the things I want to accomplish? . . . Management is efficiency in climbing the ladder of success; leadership determines whether the ladder is leaning against the right wall."[3] Another example: "Managers abound but leaders are still at a premium. Managers manage inventories, supplies, data. They are numbers crunchers. Leaders catalyze, stretch and enhance people . . . managers push and direct. Leaders pull and expect."[4] And, most succinctly: "Managers are people who do things right and leaders are people who do the right things."[5]

This line of thinking is fundamentally flawed. There is and can be no distinction between leadership and management if you are to be effective. Direction without means is feckless, and means without direction is aimless. The two—leadership and management—are inseparable. All the streamlining, cost-cutting, and reorganization in the world will do you little good if you are marching in the wrong direction. Increasing efficiency is no substitute for enhancing effectiveness. To be effective as a boss, to get the most out of your South, to be a bureaucratic entrepreneur, you must lead *and* manage.

All leadership and all management are a blend of directing and following, of speaking and listening. The blend can change over time or from situation to situation. As Peter Drucker has pointed out, "Listening is not a skill; it is a discipline."[6] Discipline or skill, listening is critical. This may not be obvious, for we think of leaders more as speakers than as listeners. But listening is essential to ensure that you are engaging the talents of those who work for you and that what you are proposing is viable.

Listening is one key to effectiveness. If you are a manager, many of the solutions to the problems on your desk may already exist in your organization; your principal task is to come up with the mechanisms for bringing the right people together to unlock these solutions.

Listening to your staff does *not* necessarily mean agreeing with them. It certainly does not mean being intimidated by expertise. It does mean providing access, be it in person or on paper, so staff members can make their argument. If the issue is sufficiently important, a meeting is probably a good idea. People are much more willing to show loyalty and implement a decision they opposed and just plain work hard if they have had their day in court. The easiest way to do this is to engender a culture or atmosphere where give-and-take is valued and individual views—no matter how different from the company line—are welcome.

At meetings with your staff, you sometimes have to restrain yourself from saying what you think. A boss who comes on strong at the outset of a meeting can discourage others from speaking up. This applies to any boss, even the president with his cabinet. In one of the first meetings after the Iraqi invasion of Kuwait, before U.S. policy had been set, George Bush decided not to speak until all the others had spoken lest he somehow discourage any point of view from being articulated. Bush believed the Iraqis had to be ousted, but had he spoken first, he would have had no way of knowing whether subsequent comments by his staff advocating this same approach represented their true opinions or only what they thought he wanted to hear.

Sometimes a leader has to disagree with advisors and colleagues; sometimes the search for consensus must be abandoned if an agenda is not to be diluted and objectives reduced to some lowest common denominator. As a rule, staff criticisms of *feasibility* should be taken more seriously than those of *desirability*. Feasibility is mostly a technical question, where expertise (often found at the staff level) is paramount, while desirability is more subjective, where judgment (reflecting the boss's vision) should count for more. Colin Powell is again worth citing on effective leadership:

> You've got to essentially say that this is where we are going, this is what we are going to do, let me start explaining to you why we have to do it, and let's see who we can get on board this train, and who is going to try to run alongside for a while, and who may never get on the train. . . . Most of the significant changes that take place in an organization have to be top-down driven or externally driven. They very seldom just emerge from those who have a commitment to the way the organization is now run. . . . You've got to eventually convince people that it is in their interest. . . . People were attacking me viciously the first year, but by the time my third year came along, they were using me as their reference point. . . . You've got to develop a consensus over time or else you pass from the scene and you haven't changed anything. Once you decide what you are going to do . . . you repeat it, you repeat it, you repeat it, you repeat it, and you just hope that history is proving you right as you go along. But you never blink.

Another Powell, in this case Sir Charles, formerly a senior advisor to Prime Minister Margaret Thatcher, recounts an example drawn from the U.S. attack on Libya in 1987—an attack that proved highly unpopular in Great Britain and strengthened the opposition to Mrs. Thatcher because of her support for the United States:

> Nobody in the government supported the Americans [in Libya], absolutely nobody. She put it to the cabinet and the only person who was vaguely in favor was Lord Hailsham, who was vaguely in favor on the somewhat eccentric grounds that his mother was American. The Foreign Office were wholeheartedly against it, believing it would lead to all our embassies in the Middle East being burned, all our interests

there ruined. But she knew it was the right thing to do and she just said, "This is what allies are for. If you're an ally, you're an ally. If one wants help, they get help." It just seemed so simple to her.

Again, the lesson is clear. The person who does not listen to the opinions of staff is foolish, and anyone who discounts facts is foolhardy. But opinions are just that, and decisions must be made by the person accountable based on his or her philosophy, agenda, and the general situation. *Consultative* leadership is one thing, *collaborative* leadership quite another.

Transitions

A central moment of your tenure as a boss and thus in your relations with your South will come when you begin. Transitions can be critical; as the ad suggests, you can only make a first impression once. Everything you do, everything you say—and how you do and say them—will be scrutinized. The people around you will feel insecure; they know they must prove themselves to you (their North) just as you must prove yourself to your own boss. Be aware, though, that people are looking for clues. James Strock, chosen by Governor Pete Wilson to head California's Environmental Protection Agency, faced this in spades:

> What's special about starting something is that anything you do is setting a precedent. You have an opportunity, you have the great difficulty of change, that's obvious enough. At the same time, you have the opportunity to institutionalize things, to get organizational inertia to work in the directions you would favor. It leads to an odd thing. It's a difficult task. You've got to focus not only on the leadership efforts and getting the governor's vision done and sold, but you've also got to simultaneously micromanage things, because these little things, like the quality of correspondence or how fast phone calls get returned or how big your office is or where you

spend your time or how open you are or are you really there
to work nights and weekends—all those things are setting
precedents and expectations.

Little things matter. Especially during transitions, but periodically thereafter, have a meeting in the office of one of your staff
members. It may seem a bit artificial, but it is worthwhile. It gives
you a chance to meet the secretaries and others who may not get
a chance to see you much; it also sends a powerful signal that you
are not remote and that you are open to ideas from others.

The style of your arrival and the transition that follows will
depend on the circumstances. Some moments call out for dramatic change—say, after a major scandal or failure that precipi-
tated your arrival, or after an election in which the winning side
gained a mandate for change. Nowhere is this approach better
demonstrated than by Eddie Murphy in the 1982 Paramount
movie *48 Hours*. Murphy walks into a country and western bar, not
accustomed to seeing black faces and even less accustomed to
being bossed around by one. He breaks a few bottles and a few
heads, announces that there is a new sheriff in town (rather ironic,
in that he portrays a felon on a two-day pass), and demands their
cooperation. This is one way of signaling change.

Dick Cheney used elements of this technique early in his tenure
as George Bush's secretary of defense. When the air force chief of
staff, Lawrence Welch, was reported to be lobbying Congress on
behalf of a weapons system whose future was still under review by
Cheney and Bush, Cheney publicly rebuked him for "freelancing."
It sent a clear message that the new civilian secretary, despite his
lack of military experience, would not countenance disobedience.

John Payton, in taking over the District of Columbia's legal
office in 1991, found an office "that was in unbelievable depths of
morale problems. It had insufficient personnel. It wasn't appreciated by another part of the government. The courts disrespected
the office. It didn't know what its mission was." A major shakeup
was obviously needed, so Payton brought in new staff members,
instituted regular, focused staff meetings, brought under one roof

personnel who had been dispersed among more than a dozen sites, reorganized, and redefined the office's mission.

Elaine Chao, hired to run United Way of America in the wake of a public scandal that forced out her predecessor after more than two decades in office, walked into an explosive situation she described as "a combination of a death in the family and a natural disaster wrapped into one." The organization was in a state of shock. Many employees had resigned; many of those remaining were afraid for their futures, unsure they had acted responsibly in the past, and skeptical of this relatively young woman (she was not yet forty) who most recently had been the Peace Corps director.

She decided to confront her staff and her situation the moment she arrived in November 1992. On her first day, she called an all-staff meeting in the building's atrium and thanked them for keeping the organization alive during this difficult period. She asked them to keep an open mind toward her, promising that she would be honest with them. She promised as well to share the good news and the bad, emphasizing that the organization's recovery would take time and effort—theirs and hers alike.

This speech was an effective hybrid of support tinged with realism. By what Chao said and the way she said it, she sent an unmistakable signal that new leadership had arrived and that the previous president's way of doing business was a thing of the past. Above all, her comments articulated a clear call for change in a context where anything less would have been inadequate.

In other situations, the Eddie Murphy approach may not be right. Long after the transition is over, you will still need the support of your organization. If you are simply replacing someone who moved on for one reason or another, if you are filling the shoes of someone perceived as successful, or if you are an unpopular, controversial, or unfamiliar choice who needs to prove yourself, you may want to start quietly and slowly. It may serve your interests best to project a message of continuity, to present yourself as someone who will concentrate on listening more than lecturing.

George Bush, who ran the CIA, the Republican National Committee, and the U.S. Liaison Office in China before becoming vice president and then president, argues for a nonconfrontational transition as the best way to get the most out of those who work for you:

> You need to know in life what you don't know. You need to have that figured out pretty well. Because people know more than you do and know it, and if they think you think you know everything, why, you'll have a rougher road. I've seen people go in there where they think they can push around people who know more than they do. You've got to give people credit for what they know or have done or [who] have accomplished a lot. If you've just gotten appointed to something and place yourself automatically over all those [people] and make little dictates out there about this is the way it is without any reference to the knowledge of others, why, you're going to fail. You're going to be less effective.

As is often the case, no single rule applies to all situations. The style and tenor of any transition must be tailored to the circumstances; your first order of business is to decide whether a message of continuity or change needs to be sent to those both inside and outside the organization. In either case, change for the sake of change is not recommended. And even if you opt for change, avoid making it any more confrontational than is necessary.

Hiring Choices

Choices involving personnel will come back to help you—or haunt you—countless times every day. The people who work for you can make you look good or bad. They can make your burden lighter or heavier. As L. William Seidman, the former head of the Federal Deposit Insurance Corporation (FDIC), has written, "No executive can succeed without good people. Good staff cannot save a

bad executive, but bad staff can pull down an otherwise compe-
tent one."[7]

Personnel decisions have a "multiplier" effect. You make only
one decision—whether to hire or keep an individual; once on
board, that person will make thousands of decisions that will
affect your reputation, impact, and effectiveness. So take the time
available—or make the time—to choose wisely. Brent Scowcroft
reports that he spent 80 percent of the two months that he had
between being appointed and taking up the job of national security advisor focusing on personnel issues. Stuart Eizenstat, Jimmy
Carter's chief domestic policy advisor and, under Bill Clinton,
U.S. ambassador to the European Community and an undersec-
retary of state, says much the same thing: "The first thing I
wanted to accomplish, which I did, was to have the absolutely best
staff that I could get, because I felt I couldn't accomplish anything substantively or procedurally unless I had a first-rate staff."
Unfortunately, not everyone has this luxury. Former treasury secretary W. Michael Blumenthal complained that of the 120,000
employees in his department, he could select only twenty-five![8]
Usually, however, you have some choice, if not at the start, then
over time as career cycles generate turnover. Take advantage of
whatever choice you get.

Try to hire people who are smarter than you are. Do not be worried that you will be overshadowed by your aides; if they do well,
you look good. At a minimum, you will get the credit for being sufficiently smart to have found them and taken them on. As
Machiavelli told his prince:

> The first criterion of the character of a prince is the kind of
> men he has about him. When they are loyal and capable, the
> prince may be judged wise; for he has known how to recog-
> nize their competence and their capacity for loyalty to him-
> self. When they are of a lesser stamp, a negative opinion will
> be formed about him, too; for the basic error is his for having
> selected them.[9]

But intelligence—or even intelligence and loyalty—cannot dictate your choice. Look for people who complement (rather than compliment) your own talents; rarely is it wise to duplicate your own strengths and weaknesses in those you hire. Thus if you are from outside the organization, you might want to find someone from within who has a good institutional memory. This was my strategy at the White House; I retained one person who had worked for my predecessor, and I always hired deputies who were on detail (loan) from one of the principal agencies involved in my work, such as the Departments of State or Defense or the CIA.

If your job has a few core areas of responsibility, you probably will not be equally proficient in all of them. Here again, find someone to compensate for you. You may have decided to concentrate on one set of issues and allow other matters in your purview to take a back seat. Assign these subordinate issues to a deputy, choosing someone who has the necessary interest and experience. Or your job may require a set of skills that you lack, such as language or technical or analytical skills. Your goal, ultimately, is to assemble a team configured to handle all possible tasks, thus allowing you the freedom and flexibility to focus where you want.

Personal considerations also count. Most people spend more of their waking hours with their officemates than with their friends and family. So pay attention to chemistry. It should not be the only consideration—you need not be friends with your staff, and beyond a certain point you probably ought not to be—but personality and "fit" should not be ignored. Work can and should be enjoyable, and an environment in which you and your subordinates do not get along is unlikely to be productive.

Political considerations should count for less. If you work in the public sector, you will sometimes be pressured to hire certain people to assuage or pay off important constituencies, especially if your appointment was controversial. Ron Brown, whose election to the chairman of the Democratic National Committee in 1988 was not universally welcomed, began by trying to hire people perceived as being more conservative than he. He quickly jettisoned this approach in favor of talent and people he felt comfortable with. As he put it, "I recruited my team and made people comfortable with me, rather than using the team to make people comfortable with me." Depending on the individuals suggested, such pressure may not be worth resisting. The quality of the people and their ability to complement you—in which political considerations play only a part—should be paramount. Also, realize that any credit you get for taking on the "right" person will fade quickly; results will soon become the only criterion by which you are measured, even by those who pressed you to hire certain people in the first place.

If possible, interview potential staff members to see how they handle themselves. Give them an opportunity to demonstrate how they think, speak, and write. You should also speak to their former bosses and review their letters of recommendation. Although written evaluations mean less and less—access to files and fear of lawsuits have taken their toll on candor—they are still worth reading, and faint praise can be a signal that something is amiss.

Closely related is the question of whom to keep, for rarely will you walk into a situation in which you do not inherit at least a few people. It often makes sense to keep some people around, at least initially, so that you can benefit from their experience and institutional memory. This will also give you a chance to rate their talents and to see how well you work together. Beware of keeping everybody, however, especially if you plan to set a new course: not only may you have more people than you really need; leaving an existing staff in place signals continuity, not change. It also deprives you of bringing in people you have already worked with, whose talent and loyalty are known quantities.

The District of Columbia's former corporation counsel John Payton makes a good case for bringing in some men and women from the outside to stimulate the career bureaucracy, at the same time keeping a number of career people with a sense of the past who will probably still be there after you have departed:

The things that have mattered the most in this job have been the people I brought from the outside. Because it has made the good people on the inside much better. And it has made them want to be sharper. And it's not just competition; but it is a completely different sensibility, of someone who isn't actually fighting to keep their job at someone else's expense. It's very, very healthy. You wouldn't want everybody from the outside, because there is valuable institutional knowledge. But it really matters.

The question of whom to keep often arises when political appointees begin a job and find themselves with a staff comprising mostly or entirely civil servants. If careerists are sometimes unhappy with what they perceive to be the bias or incompetence of their new boss—after I had served in the Pentagon for more than a year, I was still referred to as "Christmas help" by one military man—political appointees are notoriously wary of career people, fearing careerists will resist change for reasons of ideology, laziness, or both.

My own experience (and that of almost everyone I have talked with) is that generalizations are invalid, that there are talented, loyal people to be found in large organizations alongside people who are neither, and people ought to be given a chance to perform before you give up on them, try to force them out, or work around them. Also, keep in mind that some tension is unavoidable; within bounds it may even be beneficial, if it results from serious debate over the means and ends of policy. In the end, you will want your South to be a mix—of insiders and outsiders, political appointees and careerists, and experts and generalists.

Organizing Your Staff

How to structure your staff is another basic issue. Take some time before acting. Diagnose (or ask some individual or team to diagnose) whether resources are being matched correctly to tasks and whether tasks are being carried out as efficiently as they might be. Ask whether each layer and each person involved in a given task adds value; question whether procedures really serve a constructive purpose. In short, make sure it's broken before you fix it.

Reorganizations are always time consuming. They also use up political capital and tend to make matters worse before (if ever) they make things better. Beware of overreacting to what seem to be structural problems; sometimes a change in personnel or operating procedures will suffice. In the words of one skeptic, "Reorganization is like castor oil—sometimes useful in moderation, though producing drastic side effects if too much is swallowed."[10]

Colin Powell shares this feeling.

> I avoid reorganizations like the plague. They are something you do *to* somebody rather than *for* somebody. Lots of energy lost, lots of gnashing [of teeth], and so I try to chop off extraneous pieces or perhaps glue something new on, but I very seldom throw all the boxes up. I don't find that terribly useful. You are not around long enough to suffer the consequences or reap the benefits.

Structural change is a means to an end, not an end in itself; there are other, often better, ways to influence an organization and leave your mark. Performance is what matters.[11]

As a general rule, the larger your staff, the greater your range of choice in its design. You should oversee the entire operation; you can delegate day-to-day responsibility for some part of your area to others, but they should still report to and through you. Avoid allowing anyone to become so independent or unobserved that you are later surprised by what they are (or are not) doing. You are responsible for all that goes on in your domain, so you need to remain in the know. You need a reporting system that allows you to play some defense while you focus on offense. Remember, the goal is to allow yourself the freedom to focus on your priorities in a manner that does not cut you off from information. You want to be able to see opportunities or problems early enough to exploit the former and deal with the latter.

The matter of a deputy (if you have one) deserves special mention, for people use deputies differently. Your deputy can be your alter ego, included in all important meetings with your boss and your staff, someone who can step into your position without missing a beat. Alternatively, a deputy can be simply another subordinate with a set of responsibilities that you prefer to delegate. A third approach, of course, is to blend the two. A strong case, though, can be made for using the first kind of deputy, a true alter ego. Using a deputy as just another staff resource deprives you of a sometimes invaluable asset and denies the organization a clear leader when you are away. Robert Gates, a former number two at both the CIA and the National Security Council before heading the CIA, is a firm believer in the "co-equal" deputy:

> A deputy is able to function most effectively when the principal is prepared to view the deputy as an alter ego—that the deputy is to be involved in everything that the principal is involved in, the deputy knows everything that the principal knows. There is total sharing so that at any given time, if the principal is sick or out of town, the deputy can immediately step in. The other virtue . . . is that the deputy [can] give the principal a sanity check on virtually everything he does. Somebody else who presumably is independent enough to say "whoops, this is a big mistake."

Hale Champion, who was the deputy to Joseph Califano, Jimmy Carter's secretary of health, education and welfare, also firmly believes in a strong number two. His description of his relationship with Califano is revealing:

> All the people told Califano one thing. "Joe, you have to have somebody who will fight with you." Joe eats people alive. He's very hard on people; it was a very conscious recommendation for the people around him and a conscious choice by him to have somebody who would tell him he was full of shit on a

regular basis. . . . He wanted somebody who would tell him when they thought he was wrong and to fight with him about it. He knew how big a job it was and he wanted somebody who could simply say, "I'm going to be busy with this, so you do that." Joe and I averaged having lunch together three or four times a week in which we just told each other what the other one was doing. We talked about almost everything. Usually, when either one of us would have somebody over for lunch, the other one would sit in.

As is the case with any hire, the choice of a deputy should reflect much more than personal chemistry. Robert Reich's reaction to the person he asked to become his deputy at the Labor Department contains more than a little wisdom:

I wouldn't say he makes me comfortable. He's not a teddy bear. He doesn't smile much. I'd be more comfortable with someone like me—a short Jewish academic who likes to indulge in political-economic theory and grand historic visions. But I have to tell myself that the choice of deputy isn't about comfort. That's the mistake made by too many who move into positions like mine: They want to replicate themselves. Or they bring in old friends. It seems safer that way—after all, you know what you're getting and you can count on their loyalty—but it's also more dangerous, because an old friend or someone who shares the same personality traits isn't likely to be able to see what you can't see or do what you can't do. You share the same disabilities. I need someone who *isn't* like me. And that means a hard-ass who will hold people accountable, demand results, and fire them if they don't produce. With me in charge of day-to-day operations, people would be holding hands in a big circle, expressing their innermost feelings.[12]

If you have enough people, an additional option is to establish one or several people "off line" with a specific responsibility—say, speechwriting or planning or technical analysis—who report directly to you or a deputy. Overlapping jurisdictions can make for some turmoil and friction in the ranks, but, if kept in check, they can introduce some healthy competition and oversight.

Creating special teams can be valuable in handling a high-priority project—the Clinton administration's effort to reinvent government, entitled the National Performance Review, represented a decision by Vice President Al Gore to replicate an approach commonly used in the business world. According to Philip Lader, for a time the deputy director of the Office of Management and Budget (OMB):

> [Gore] made the conscious decision that he wanted to follow the General Motors–Saturn model of plucking people out of the bowels of the organization at every level to have insights from people who worked with it where the rubber meets the road. . . . It would [also] be more sellable because the people who would have to implement it have been part of the initial line drawings and the blueprints.

Special groups can also be useful in managing a crisis; here the Kennedy administration's Executive Committee, established to oversee the Cuban Missile Crisis, and the Bush administration's "Small Group," which managed the 1990–91 Persian Gulf crisis, among others, come to mind. So, too, does the Clinton administration's use of "war rooms" to handle significant votes. Such structures allow those with a narrow but high-priority focus to pursue an issue without having to worry at the same time about other responsibilities. You need to be sure, though, that these ad hoc creations draw on and communicate with the standing bureaucracy (and any other powers in a position to affect their work) lest they sow confusion and undermine their own effectiveness as well as that of other individuals and groups with related mandates. Failure to do just this is one of the principal factors accounting for the failure of the Clinton administration's health reform effort.

A related question is how to structure your staff to ensure that you receive the best possible advice. Effective decisionmaking requires timely and accurate information; a mechanism for ensuring that problems and opportunities get placed on the agenda; the participation of the "right" people, in terms of a need to be involved and appropriate rank; a canvassing of all possible policy choices with a rigorous but fair assessment of their probable costs, feasibility, and consequences; an opportunity for recommendations to be made by those with a legitimate stake in the outcome; the clear communication of a decision once it is made; and the provision for and oversight of necessary implementation.[13]

This set of requirements is, of course, somewhat idealized. But any system that does not attempt to do all these things well is destined to perform poorly. Indeed, without such a structure, you are likely to end up with a whole that is less than its parts. The productivity of talented people can be squandered by poor structures and procedures for policy development and decisionmaking.

Decisionmaking Choices

Even if he or she has little control over personnel or organizational structure, almost any manager can shape the process by which decisions are made. Staff structures for decisionmaking tend to fall into one of three types: centralized management, multiple advocacy, and adhocracy.

Centralized management involves creating a small team of people close to you who filter all that comes to you and in some cases originate all that comes to you. This approach maintains tight control over who knows what, which might be essential if secrecy is truly required. If your staff members are sufficiently talented, centralized management can ensure good work; it can also yield new efficiency in areas of an organization that have been sluggish. This approach is sometimes preferred by political appointees who mistrust or do not value the large career bureaucracies they inherit; both the National Security Council under Henry Kissinger and the State Department under James Baker reflected this bias.

The risk in centralized management is that certain issues get ignored and too many resources are left idle, which can create problems when decisions require implementation. A long-term weakness is that it tends to put down few roots: when those involved depart, the institution tends to revert to the status quo ante. Robert Gates's depiction of the CIA makes this clear:

> The only way that you make lasting change in a bureaucracy is to set an objective, tell the senior managers of the institution where you want to go, and then make them a part of the process of getting there so that they come to believe that the solution is their idea. And the bureaucracy assimilates it and defends it as its own rather than as something imposed from above. That's what I did with all the task forces in changing the intelligence community. . . . In every case, I made the task force report and the recommendations available and then, in a second stage, my proposed decision memo available to anybody in the agency or the intelligence community who wanted to see it before it was issued. And every single decision memo I wrote was influenced by the comments I got from the troops. Some of the things I did were in fact things that [former Director Stansfield] Turner tried to do, but Stan simply imposed them from above, said "This is the way it's going to be done, and screw you," and all those changes walked out the door right behind him.

Multiple advocacy resembles a wagon wheel, with all the spokes leading to and from the center. Two examples of this approach are the National Security Council under Brent Scowcroft and the National Economic Council under Robert Rubin. In both examples, all persons and agencies with a legitimate stake in the issues are invited to participate in the policymaking process—although not necessarily in the decision about which policy to pursue, something reserved for the president or his designated representative.

The advantage of multiple advocacy is that all resources are tapped and that implementation tends to go more smoothly because people understand what was decided and why. However, this approach is also time consuming, is prone to leaks, and requires talented and fair-minded people at the center who ensure that due process is dispensed. They must be sufficiently disciplined so that their desire to be advocates takes a back seat to their responsibility for ensuring fairness. Brent Scowcroft describes the challenge he faced:

> I had three responsibilities to the President. The first was to acquaint him with the essence of issues, what the issue really was and the different perspectives. If we were going to have an NSC meeting or an informal group to discuss Topic A, I would try to get him up on subject A so that he could put the arguments into a framework and thus usefully analyze it. Second, after I'd done that, I owed him the benefit of my own views on it, while at the same time explaining to the best of my ability and objectivity other people's views. Unless the other members of the system are confident that you would give their views a fair shake, the system tends to break down, and they will insist on going to the President on every issue, whatever it is, because they don't trust that their views will be adequately presented. Third, after he made a decision, I'd do my best to make sure the decision was implemented in the way he had made it.

Alas, few people can play the game and be a referee at the same time. As Roger Porter, a former White House aide, describes it: "The role of the honest broker in a multiple advocacy model is twofold: it's not simply dispensing due process, but it's [also] exercising quality control. And that often means a more activist role in advancing initiatives and in advocating certain courses of action. And hopefully doing it in a way that it doesn't compromise the perception of you as a dispenser of due process." What is required is not simply a broker but an "honest balancer," someone who dispenses due process but who also is willing and able to intervene so that the principal gets the best advice even if none of the participating agencies produces it. When individuals are not up to this challenge—and few are—the process degenerates. The Carter and Reagan National Security Councils come to mind; both operations often suffered "gridlock" as well as a lack of coordination and consistency.

Adhocracy is the third approach. It does not depend on any set pattern for making decisions and has the advantage of avoiding the slowness and the lack of creativity that can characterize large bureaucracies. It provides great flexibility to the decisionmaker. Adhocracy was the favored management style of Franklin Roosevelt and John Kennedy—and, more recently, of Bill Clinton.

The problem with adhocracy is that it places great demands on the person at the center. Those who use this approach are also prone to losing sight of priorities and to erring when it comes to implementation. Arthur Schlesinger's portrait of FDR is revealing: "His favorite technique was to keep grants of authority incomplete, jurisdictions uncertain, charters overlapping. The result of this competitive theory of administration was often confusion and exasperation on the operating level."[14]

Adhocracy can also be a real problem during crises, when the need for clarity increases sharply. There is less time to sort out any confusion, less margin for error, and higher stakes. And although special arrangements can be instituted, it is virtually impossible to introduce discipline overnight into an environment lacking clear lines of authority and defined areas of responsibility. The difficulties encountered by city officials who tried to restore order in Los Angeles during the 1992 riots and in New York in the wake of the Crown Heights incident in 1992 offer persuasive evidence of just this point.[15]

Each of these approaches to decisionmaking has its strengths and weaknesses; there is no best way for all people or all organizations at all times. And no system, no matter how well designed or staffed, can eliminate the need for the decisionmaker's judgment. Experts can be wrong; individuals and even entire agencies or governments can become victims of "groupthink" or a set of shared assumptions. Hardly anyone in the U.S. government predicted Khrushchev would place missiles in Cuba. Few in Israel in the autumn of 1973 believed that the Arabs would start a war, just as few in the Middle East or the United States (myself included) thought Saddam Hussein would invade Kuwait in the summer of 1990.

The best way to protect yourself from the perils of fixed mindsets or the biases often found in analysis and prescription is to ask questions, first of yourself, then of others. Do you have all the information that is available? Is there any relevant history you need to know? Are you speaking to all those with real insight into and knowledge of this question? Is the information you are getting in any way biased by what courses of action people favor? Have you been presented with a full range of options, including the status quo? Are the options viable, both politically and operationally? What is the expected cost and benefit of each option? What assumptions are being made? How sensitive or vulnerable are the analyses and recommendations to any of these assumptions? What is the worst possible outcome, and how likely is it?

You can also protect yourself from avoidable errors through regular department reviews of policy and basic assumptions. Still another option is to create "red teams" of individuals (possibly from your West) selected for their known contrary positions, who are then given access to all available information, asked to produce their views, and allowed to debate with those representing the existing policy positions. The goal is to build bulwarks in order to avoid allowing a particular mindset to take hold and blind you to new realities.

But even with the best advice and the best decisionmaking systems, mistakes will be made. There are always unforeseen developments and unknown factors. But a good decisionmaking process should minimize the unexpected and leave you in a position to say that you made the best decision possible based on everything that could be known and measured at the time. If the results are good, so much the better, but poor results alone do not mean that the decision or the process was flawed.

Being a Successful Boss

When it comes to managing subordinates, there is no universal rule other than this: *ordering staff to do something ought to be a last resort*. Orders create resentment and rarely stimulate quality or efficiency. What Richard Neustadt has written about presidents—that "command is but a method of persuasion, not a substitute, and not a suitable method for everyday employment"—is even more true for everyone else.[16] Mark McCormack makes a related point: "Being the boss is more a question of adding value than exercising power . . . there's a difference between being the boss and being bossy."[17] Colin Powell agrees: Management "is more than just the ability to order people to do things, which we [in the military] of course can do. But that isn't management. Ordering is ordering. Management is different. Leadership is different." Often the best bosses, the ones who get the most out of those who work for them, are precisely those who do *not* act in ways that call to mind traditional images of the boss.

Not surprisingly, Machiavelli has a good deal to say on this subject. He argues that it is preferable to be feared than loved, if one must choose between them, but that best of all is to be feared but not hated. He warns against traits that will bring the prince into contempt, including fickleness, frivolity, cowardliness, and lack of resolution. "Against these the prince should be on his guard as he would against the plague." Instead, Machiavelli suggests that the prince do his best to lend his actions the appearance of greatness, high-spiritedness, seriousness, and strength.[18]

Perhaps the most important thing a boss or manager can do is attempt to create an environment in which individuals feel encouraged to come forward with their ideas, no matter how different they may be from the company or party line. You want from your South just what you owe your North. A boss needs to encourage this less obvious dimension of "loyalty up," in part for self-protection. Robert Gates makes this abundantly clear:

> Finding people in government who will tell you what they think in very blunt terms is very difficult. . . . The problem is that when you've got a hundred things to do, and you are working a hundred issues at the same time, somebody who sends you a comment or comments to you on something in a way that takes the sharp edges off, that rounds it out, often if you are in a hurry or busy, it will just go right over you. You need somebody to hit you with a two-by-four, to say "This is a problem. You are about to fuck up. Or somebody else is about to fuck up." And so I would always have at the end of my checklist what I call sanity checks: a handful of people, it could be one on an issue, it could be three or four, that I would insist have a look at the document or proposal before I would sign off on it. Every senior principal needs somebody like that. . . . The manager who conveys signals that that's not welcome, that plain speaking and disagreeing are not welcome, is in desperate jeopardy.

An intellectually open environment is also the best way to encourage the highest possible performance from those who work for you. People who feel included, who feel that their participation and contributions are respected and valued, are far more likely to work hard than those who feel neglected. This is especially true in the public sector, where a manager's ability to bestow monetary awards or even promotions is often limited.

How best to do this? Inclusion in a fair process of decisionmaking is the single best approach available. George Bush adopted this as his model:

> You just can't keep strong-willed people happy every minute. In our case, for example, we had Brent [Scowcroft] oozing around between these guys, working it out and sparing me a hell of a lot of heartburn. But every once in a while he had to

come in there and say, "Look, you've got to make a decision, [Defense Secretary Dick] Cheney wants to do this, [Secretary of State James] Baker wants to do that, here's what the CIA people think, what do you want me to do?" And then you make it. But if you've done it properly, you don't have the loser in an internecine battle like that thinking that his views weren't even heard.

Another way to get the most out of your South is to reach out, thus avoiding the dangers of limiting yourself to an inner circle of advisors. Demonstrating to people that their ideas and recommendations are welcome can be done in little ways—walking around and being seen, opening the doors of the executive suite. It can also be done by giving people access to you. Keeping staff happy is not the only reason to adopt an open management style. You can also help yourself more directly by developing new sources of information. Prime Minister Margaret Thatcher was known to write notes to herself and place them in her handbag after consulting one or another member of an informal set of friends and advisors. Her staff came to recognize that arguing with what emerged from her handbag was usually futile. Hale Champion similarly argues for an informal approach when gathering necessary information:

> You don't go by hunch, you try to assemble information, but you try to assemble informal information, good judgment, people you trust, get the stuff from them, and then you use the data systems to check you out and to keep track and to do some other stuff. So you need them both. . . . If you've got nine levels out there, which you frequently do, everybody knows what happens about the story that comes up through nine levels, all the elements of doubt and self interest that go into changing what you end up hearing. I have one simple rule in every large organization: I call anybody I want to. It may be asking about something in the data. I try to call directly to the place that I think is the source. If I read a memorandum, I don't call the person whose name is on

the memorandum, I call and say, "Who wrote the memorandum?" I don't care about the guy who sent it to me; what I care about is the guy who wrote it. And the understanding in all these organizations is that when I talk to somebody like that, they are responsible for everybody between me and them knowing we had the conversation.

Another way to provide access is to establish a special track for memos to ensure that they can reach you and that they will be heard—the equivalent of a suggestions box. At the State Department, for example, this track is called the Dissent Channel. All staff members in an organization should be able to send in their thinking, even if their immediate supervisors disagree, without cost to their career. A dissent channel is not for casual use, but in special circumstances it can prove valuable. Even in normal times, simply the existence of such a channel provides comfort and reassurance to your staff.

The Boss as Educator

Responding to written work is essential. Turning your office into a bureaucratic black hole of Calcutta (or a branch of the National Archives) is as demoralizing for staff as it is inefficient for you. Mary Jo Bane, formerly the commissioner of New York State's Department of Social Services, makes the point that the best way to effect change can be indirect—by what you write in the margin of a memo or what you say at a meeting. Take notice of those who have the courage to take you on and make clear to everyone that this is respected. Richard Armitage, a former Defense Department official, has this to say on the responsibility of a boss to communicate to those who work for him:

> Always respond to staff. Always, always, always . . . it's absolutely essential that a staff officer get an answer. It doesn't have to be a yes or no. But they have to know that their material is being read. . . . It's frustrating in a whole host of ways

not to get responses back. It leads people to be dissatisfied, to say "Look, I'm working my butt off giving this guy my thoughts and I don't even get a check mark that it's been read." At a minimum, it is important to respond, even if the only response is, This is a good point, or I don't agree with this point, or I read this, and it's helpful with me, it's getting in my mind. I may disagree with it, but it's in there. And the effect on you as a staff officer is to encourage you to continue. So we always responded.

It helps to think of yourself as a teacher, in a version of the fishes and loaves parable: better to instruct how to fish than to provide a meal. As a manager, you are better off explaining why you want something done a certain way or why you edited a memo or speech the way you did; avoid taking actions without explanation or ordering that something be done without providing some kind of justification. This method will take more time in the short run, but in the long run teaching will help morale and enable you to get more and better work out of your staff—all while sparing yourself time and effort.

Every employee needs something different from a superior in order to perform up to his or her potential. Some need close supervision, including frequent and detailed explanations of what is required. Others need only the most general guidance and will get it done right. Pay close attention to signals: studying your South is no less important for effectiveness than studying your North. In time, you will learn the most useful approach with each of the people who work for you.

Some staff members require great amounts of praise while others merit more than a little criticism. Again, there is no universal rule, although praise is rarely unwelcome. Criticism, depending on how it is meted out, can be useful; I would only suggest that critical comments be made in private.

What you ask of your staff must be tailored as well. Some people are wonderful at speech writing; others are not. It makes little sense to give an inexperienced writer the assignment to draft an important public address unless there is a great deal of time to improve the drafts and you have the luxury of turning the exercise into a teaching experience. Others are good with think pieces; some are unable to conceptualize but are wonderful at juggling twenty-five small, operational issues. Come to know your staff, their strengths and weaknesses, and take advantage of the former while you work to shore up the latter.

It is generally better to give direction early. If you assign a staff member to produce a report on a complex issue, ask to see some evidence of their progress—an outline or a rough draft—sooner rather than later. Nothing is less productive than having a subordinate slave away on a project for a long time only to hand in something that is not at all what you had in mind. It is a waste of everyone's time and terrible for morale.

Strive to be consistent and even somewhat predictable. Most good employees consider it hard enough to work for someone under the best of circumstances, but they find it nearly impossible if their bosses have wild mood swings or frequently change their mind about what they want or expect. A boss who is too willing to change course, especially on important issues, also risks losing respect, for such behavior demonstrates a lack of conviction and a lack of purpose that will confuse and over time demoralize a staff.

Remember, too, that whether you mean to or not, you will manage by example. Subordinates notice how hard you work, whether corners are being cut, what is truly respected and valued. Managing is in some ways like parenting, and what you do can have a far greater impact than what you say. It also helps if you are willing to join in; as Condoleezza Rice points out, "The worst thing you can do as a boss is have your people do things that you're not willing to do, whether it's stay late at night or take and transcribe notes. If you're not willing to do it, you shouldn't ask anybody else to do it."

As Ohio's attorney general, Lee Fisher inherited an enormous backlog of cases involving compensation claims for crime victims. Every person—regardless of rank or defined responsibility—in his thousand-person office was asked to help clear the backlog. Some 300 employees, lawyers and support staff, volunteered, taking the necessary training and going through the case files. So did Fisher. As result, the backlog was eliminated (making many citizens happy), and a new sense of teamwork came to exist in the office.

Ross Sandler, once New York City's maverick transportation commissioner, says:

> City people, people who work in city governments, are very well attuned to which way the wind is blowing. If it's going to be politics, they'll do politics. If it's going to be professional management where promotion is done by merit, they'll do that. They are very cautious, they have incredible antennae, they know exactly how to survive in the system, they all hate the civil service, they all have been burned one way or another. So what I tried to do is convey to them that this is going to be an honest, professional management; promotions and merit raises would come if you did a good job, and praise would come.

Managing by example has its limits, however. Just because the boss works eighteen hours a day does not mean such a schedule is appropriate or useful for everyone else. Each person needs to develop—or be encouraged to develop—an approach that fits the position and is suited to the individual's skills and talents.

Last, do not forget good management when it comes to your secretary. Your secretary may constitute most or all of your South, yet all too often secretaries are taken for granted and not recognized as subordinates who require the same attention, feedback, guidance, and loyalty as other employees. Remember, the person who answers your phones, greets visitors, and prepares correspondence and memos affects how you are perceived. Moreover, your secretary can become an added resource—as a researcher, say, or a letter writer—if you take the time and make the effort to develop and encourage him or her. Job descriptions can be created—and often expanded—leaving both boss and secretary more satisfied with the result.

Management Tools

Staff meetings are a familiar management tool. One approach is to meet frequently; some managers like to meet each morning, after people have had time to drink their coffee and think about the day. This is a good chance to hear what people have on their plates, to react to any news, and to provide some guidance. It is best if these meetings are fairly short, for everyone has work to do. One general in the Pentagon had everybody stand—he even called his morning staff meetings "standups"—in order to encourage people not to talk any more than they absolutely had to.[19]

Morning staff meetings can also provide a setting in which staff members can interact. William Kristol, the chief of staff to Vice President Dan Quayle, came to appreciate this feature:

> Sharing information is extremely important. It is underrated. Simply making sure that everyone who needs to know knows things is a big task in government. We had effective meetings where nothing was decided and I didn't say a word, but at least the legislative guy told the press guy what he had to know to answer questions, and the domestic policy guy found out information from the legislative guy. It's very evident that everyone gets so wrapped up around their own little ball of wax. . . . You have to try very hard to pull people together. The centrifugal forces—the forces that push you out—are stronger.

A second sort of staff meeting is less about going down lists or exchanging perishable information than about developing ideas. The meeting can be regular—say, once a month—although this can be artificial. It is often better to schedule a meeting of this type when you or one of your key staff members desire one. Such meetings can be devoted to discussing an issue—a problem, an opportunity, or both—or to taking a step back in an effort to gain perspective and evaluate your broad direction. Think of this kind of meeting as a form of retreat without all the hassle of going off into the woods and sleeping on the hard ground while fending off the bugs.

Similar to regular staff meetings are Daily Activity Reports (DARs, or WARs, if the reports are weekly). These are short, end-of-the-day (or week) informal memos from the ranks to the boss or from the periphery to the center describing recent events or noting any developments that might be worth more time and focus. DARs can be a way of complementing the morning or end-of-day staff meeting or even substituting for one. If you require DARs from your staff, mark them up and send them back first thing in the morning. Once everyone adapts to this system, DARs are a quick and easy way to keep in touch with your staff and to minimize the chance of being surprised. Staff members tend to groan at first under the weight of having to do what looks like make-work, but they quickly grow to appreciate these reports because they provide access to and quick feedback from the top.

Different from regular staff meetings but no less important is a mechanism to ensure that your staff knows what they need to know. Invariably, you will be involved in meetings or conversations in which information is exchanged and decisions made that will affect the work of people to your South. Unless you tell your staff members about these meetings, however, they will be toiling away without the benefit of information that can make them more valuable to you, to their own staff, or in their contacts with both their East and West. Timely and thorough "debriefing," whether done in person or over the phone, is essential.

In the end, the key to being a good boss comes down to communicating by word and deed that those who work *for* you actually work *with* you. Brent Scowcroft did this as well as anyone:

> I felt I was being well served when I asked for something that was done quickly and thoughtfully, that I was reminded of things that I hadn't thought of or hadn't realized. What I wanted was expert background to my general knowledge of areas so I didn't make a mistake or do something wrong. But

I really wanted collaborators, not simply subordinates. People who could and would talk with me about larger issues as intellectual equals, not simply as a subordinate carrying out instructions to produce paper A or paper B.

Any manager or leader must communicate the sense that everyone matters, that everyone contributes, and that the ultimate success of the organization—that realization of its mission—depends on the efforts of all of its members. Colin Powell makes this clear in his description of a successful military organization:

> When it comes to Mission, we teach it and we train it in a way that it is always the big M: close with and destroy the enemy. If you are doing nothing more than going out in the motor pool this afternoon, and get dirty and miserable for three hours changing the transmission on a tank, or draining the sump pump of an engine, that's important. That goes toward the big M. If that tank doesn't do what it is supposed to do, when it is supposed to do it, you may fail the big M. So everything is important. The guy flipping hamburgers for lunch is participating in the big M. . . . Everybody's mission is tied to everybody else's mission so that the whole thing constitutes a whole.

Delegation

There is no better way to introduce the subject of delegation than by quoting from President Abraham Lincoln's letter of April 1864 to General Ulysses S. Grant:

> Not expecting to see you again before the Spring Campaign opens, I wish to express, in this way, my entire satisfaction with what you have done up to this time, so far as I understand it. The particulars of your plans I neither know or seek to know. You are vigilant and self-reliant; and pleased with this, I wish not to obtrude any constraints or restraints upon you. While I

am very anxious that any great disaster, or the capture of our men in great numbers, shall be avoided, I know these points are less likely to escape your attention than they would be mine. If there is anything wanting which is within my power to give, do not fail to let me know it. And now with a brave Army, and a just cause, may God sustain you.[20]

Few of us will ever find ourselves in shoes resembling either Lincoln's or Grant's. As a result, it is more likely that we will determine that no management issue is more vexing than delegation. Delegation should vary according to the individuals involved, the importance of the task, and the confidence that has evolved between you and your South. Some degree of delegation is essential; otherwise, you will exhaust yourself and dilute your impact as well as deny yourself the talents of your staff. But if you delegate too much, you risk losing control over what is going on and how well it is being done.

My favorite illustration of this dilemma comes from *Fortune* magazine. On September 15, 1986, *Fortune* ran a cover story entitled, "What Managers Can Learn from Manager Reagan." Ronald Reagan's secret? "Surround yourself with the best people you can find, delegate authority, and don't interfere as long as the policy you've decided upon is being carried out."[21] Seven months later, a story by the same respected journalist in the same magazine was called, "Learning from Reagan's Debacle."[22] The first piece praised Reagan's loose management style and his willingness to delegate; the second (written in the aftermath of the Iran-Contra revelations) highlighted the shortcomings of a management style that was out of touch, one that was undermined by weak supervision, unclear rules, and an absence of review. How does one get it just right?

Delegation is a subject on which the business literature has something very useful to say. The notion of "loose-tight" management translates well into the nonprofit world. One should be tight—that is, both specific and demanding—in expecting that performance is of high quality and that goals are met, but one should be loose or minimally intrusive in overseeing just how this is done. (Alas, the opposite is often the case: many people seem more concerned with not deviating from prescribed processes than with accomplishing anything of value.) It was this loose-tight philosophy that led Joseph Fernandez to institute a successful system he called "school-based management," a sort of educational decentralization effort, in Miami's public schools.[23] During the Gulf War, President Bush and his senior lieutenants were careful not to immerse themselves in the details of military operations. Rather, Bush made a conscious decision to hand over this responsibility to the armed services and so avoid President Johnson's mistake during the Vietnam War. Set standards, make the direction clear, examine results—but do not micromanage. You want to steer, but you do not want to do all the rowing yourself.

A good rule of thumb is offered by James Strock, the first person to head California's Environmental Protection Agency: "Anything I do, if it can be done equally well or better by somebody else, I'm not going to do it. I shouldn't be doing it." Delegation can free you up to focus on your agenda. Billy Webster, perhaps because he came out of the business world—before becoming chief of staff to Education Secretary Riley, he owned the Bojangles chain of fried chicken and biscuit outlets in South Carolina—has strong views on the subject. "I've seen more people screw up faster already since I've been in Washington, people who think that if you turn loose either information or authority you become less, when in fact you become more. The ability to delegate effectively is enormously important; there's too damn much to do around here to have any other attitude."

Nevertheless, delegation is easier advised than accomplished. It is difficult to let go, difficult to allow others to do what we are used to doing—and that applies whether they do it less well or better. But in the end it is essential, both for your own effectiveness—delegation allows you to focus on your priorities—and to the morale and effectiveness of your staff. Sheila Burke, the chief of staff to Senate Minority Leader Bob Dole, highlights the link between delegation and the effectiveness of your staff:

It's a difficult situation when you are the perceived boss. People want to deal with you directly. They don't want to deal with the underlings. But the underlings need that kind of reinforcement so that people will ultimately know that they are people that have to be dealt with and have to be negotiated with. I try to be very careful about not intervening or stepping into the middle of a relationship that allows my staff to get information, to develop consensus, to really go about becoming their own people in their own right. There have been times that I have had staff come and complain to me that "so-and-so won't talk to me, they'll only deal with you," and I try very much to go back to those people and say, "This is the person you need to talk with. She's keeping me informed. I'll let you know if it's not going in the right direction."

The keys to resolving the difficulties associated with delegation are several: set clear guidelines, hire good people, and establish mechanisms for monitoring what your staff is up to. In the end, how well you delegate will have much to do with how well you manage your South—and how well you fare overall.

Showing Loyalty Down

The previous chapter discussed "loyalty up," which requires that you give your boss your best counsel but carry out whatever policy is decided on even if it is not your own preference. The corresponding notion, not surprisingly, is "loyalty down," your responsibility to those who toil for you.

Loyalty down has three elements. First, you owe it to your staff to make sure they receive their fair share of the credit when the work is theirs. Second, you should shield them from criticism and attack when the responsibility is not theirs. Third, you should help them develop their skills and advance their careers even if it makes your life more difficult when they attend a training course or, worse yet, move on.

What a staff person writes or thinks frequently becomes anonymous or is appropriated as it moves up the bureaucratic ladder. Sometimes a subordinate's work bears the name of the boss. This is fine, for the boss must take responsibility for an idea if it is passed North, but it is only fair that the contribution be recognized and that praise get passed around. Sometimes this can be accomplished by noting who a memorandum is "From" in the first instance; if it passes through you to your boss, your name can be on the "Through" line, between "From" and "To."

Richard Armitage underscores the need to share credit:

> Your success is absolutely dependent upon the success of those under you. You cannot be successful unless they're successful. So be sure you're not successful at their expense. To the extent they're seen as very competent people, you're seen as even more competent. This means that you have to reach out occasionally to boost them up. At the end of the day, if you haven't brought various people up into the limelight, over time you'll find that their ability to work sixteen- and eighteen-hour days, which periodically is required, is diminished. People need to see the sunlight on occasion, to feel the heat, its good, positive warmth. A good, competent manager looks for an occasion to bring people in. Never forget your people. If I kept them there, I awarded them, or rewarded them, in some way, something big or small.

Praise means a lot. Again, the public sector rarely is able to reward excellence and effort properly. Ross Sandler describes what he did in New York in light of these constraints:

> One of the things we did was we created all sorts of events to praise workers. Not for doing exceptional jobs, but for doing their job. We gave away plaques, we had ceremonies, I would visit sites and thank everybody; I'd go out at night and watch when we were doing resurfacing at night and shake everybody's hand and say they're doing a good job—a lot of visibility. . . . We went to one ceremony and we got there, and

there was a big sign that the workers had hung up, and it said, "The workers of the East River division of bridges are proud of their work and are ready to do more."

Not being recognized can demoralize a person. In my late twenties, I was at the bottom of the bureaucratic ladder, laboring in the Pentagon basement. But I was part of a small team that had direct access to one of the top people in the building. One day this senior official took a memorandum I had written, did little more than replace my name with his, walked into the secretary's office, and said that this represented his views, which he had to write out himself given the poor performance of his staff. I determined right then that I would not work for this individual for long. I also resolved that if and when I came to have my own staff, I would never treat them as I had just been treated.

Years later, when I did have a small staff of my own, I was occasionally criticized for things they either did or failed to do. It is tempting when you are being read the riot act by your boss to try to explain the mistake away (and save your own hide) by blaming those who work for you. Do not do it. A willingness to stand by your staff is essential if you are to engender an environment where intelligent risk-taking and innovation become the norm.[24] Moreover, distancing yourself from those who work for you does not help you with your boss—you are still viewed as responsible, for it happened on your watch—and it does not help you with your staff, who feel vulnerable and betrayed. Get it right the first time, or take the heat yourself since you probably okayed it at some point. If you did not, you have a management problem—that is, you are being too lax in your oversight—and you probably need to rein in or replace one or more members of your staff. Remember the bad example of Joseph Heller's Ralph, who told the hapless Bruce Gold, "This Administration will back you all the way until it has to."[25]

In return for loyalty down, you have a right to insist on all aspects of loyalty up: honest counsel, full implementation, and complete discretion. The latter entails expecting that what was said in the office remains there; you do not want to hear—much less read about—a policy still under discussion or the gory details of a decision made.

Letting People Go

The responsibility to assist people to move on is often unwelcome, for invariably it is your best people who get the opportunity. When it happens, and it will, you should either match the offer or let the person go. The danger, of course, is that you will lose the flowers and find yourself with mostly weeds, thereby increasing the pressure to hire more good people. You will find it easier to do this if you are recognized as a boss who provides good opportunities that can serve as a springboard to even better things.

The flip side of hiring is firing. Inevitably, you will inherit people who do not make the grade. You also will hire people who do not turn out as you had hoped and expected. Either way, you will find this an awkward situation to handle. Try to address the problem as soon as it surfaces; it is unfair to the person involved—and poor management, to boot—to wait until the staff person's performance is so bad that firing seems to be the only option.[26] An early warning gives the person a chance to rectify the situation, in which case you both win: you get a better performance; the person gets a better appraisal and keeps the job.

You should thus meet with each individual who reports directly to you early to review what is expected. Periodically, you should sit down and review his or her performance; the annual review, often mandated by law, that appears on paper is not enough, especially if there are problems. Such meetings are especially important in the nonprofit world, where clear criteria for measuring performance are not always possible. A bad performance appraisal can destroy your ability to work with someone on your staff and sink his or her career.

Just as important, you have protected yourself if the situation cannot be resolved to your satisfaction. Firing someone can open a legal hornet's nest, and the best way to limit your own vulnerability as a supervisor is to document all communications so that the individual affected cannot complain about not being warned or given a fair chance. The advice of Robert White, the chief of staff to California governor Pete Wilson, is especially helpful here:

> It's not easy—ever. I know everybody says it's difficult. But it is not as hard as people say it is, as much as you dread it [if] you do it in a fair way, and you are honest with them. . . . Most people aren't honest when they fire people. They say "Oh, well, you know, gee, I'm sorry, somebody's going to have to do this," rather than "You're going to have to be let go for these reasons. And this is how far I can go in recommending you for your next job, because they are going to call me." And you set up the parameters by which they leave so that you're not just doing something that either appears to be cavalier or insensitive or, on the other hand, not being forthright and honest with them. I think you have to feel like you've done the right thing.

Conclusions

If you supervise others in an organization, your effectiveness with your North, as well as with your East and West, will be a direct result of the capacity of your South. For it is those to your South who will be drafting memos, making arguments, going to meetings, and perhaps even giving speeches on your behalf. They will shape your thinking and help you set a course of action. They represent you; they serve you. As a result, whom you hire, how you organize them, how you motivate them, how well you listen, how much you direct—all are important issues and choices. You cannot be effective if those who work for you are not. So building their effectiveness ought to be a priority. Do not make the mistake of focusing solely on substance and relegating personnel and other administrative decisions to second place.

Considerable thought must also be given to how decisions are made and implemented. Any process must ensure that people are included, that they come away with a sense of fairness, that options are thoroughly vetted, that decisions are made and everybody knows what they are, that mechanisms exist for oversight and follow-up. All of this requires that you create and support an environment that encourages people to contribute. You can do this by including your staff, reacting to what they do, delegating real responsibility, and teaching where appropriate. *Treat staff no worse and where possible better than you like to be treated and you will probably not do badly as a boss.*

Last, remember that ordering and dictating ought to be a last resort. Inspiration, motivation, example, and persuasion ought to be the principal ways of getting the most out of your South. Be both a leader and a manager if you want to be effective. Not everyone working for you should have a veto, but everyone should have a voice. This in turn requires a willingness to listen as well as a readiness to make decisions and act on them according to your own philosophy, agenda, and opportunities. Your South is your foundation, not only for your relations with your North, but for your relations East and West.

5

East:
Those with
Whom You
Work

THUS FAR WE HAVE EXPLORED relations with the North and South, up and down the chain of authority. These relations are characterized mostly by people working *for* someone else. Relations with the East involve people working *with* other people. There is little or no ability to order or command or even exert control. Persuasion is your principal tool, often the only one. Those to your East, while still in your organization or under the same umbrella, usually have their own bosses, their own staffs, their own agendas. They are like you. They are part of the enterprise, outside your span of control, but not outside your span of influence—if you go about it right.

Clashing and Cooperating with Colleagues

Democratic governments operate on the principle of shared authority; overlapping jurisdiction is the norm, not the exception. Democracy, or more accurately a republican version of democracy, in which the people act in large part through their elected and appointed representatives, is designed with checks and balances to prevent or at least hinder dramatic changes or extreme policies. Those who wrote the Constitution valued protection against tyranny above efficiency; the result is our complicated federal system, in which power is divided (or shared) among the three branches of the federal government and then again within and among various levels of national, state, and local government.

The direct consequence of this political philosophy is that the individual can accomplish very little acting alone. Others are needed to support and implement a decision; likewise, many decisions can be thwarted by those who oppose them. As a result, a good deal of one's time is devoted to bringing along colleagues, to persuading them to do what you want, or at least to support decisions once they are made.

Tension and conflict are inevitable in any bureaucracy. Organizations are composed of people, and for reasons of philosophy, personality, perspective, organizational and personal self-interest, or just about anything else you can imagine, they will clash. At one point, former White House speechwriter Peggy Noonan likened her struggles with her colleagues to a fondue pot surrounded by too many people trying to get their forks in; at another, she conjured up a different culinary image. "Think of a bunch of wonderful, clean, shining, perfectly shaped and delicious vegetables. Then think of one of those old-fashioned metal meat grinders. Imagine the beautiful vegetables being forced through the grinder and being rendered into a smooth, dull, textureless puree."[1]

This was how Noonan, a talented wordsmith, saw it. The "vegetables" were her words before her colleagues went to work on them. I expect some of her colleagues had a different view; perhaps they saw her as a chef prone to using too much spice. Indeed, I recall that one of her more dramatic and pessimistic drafts of a speech about the prospects of the West was dubbed "Darkness at Noonan" by those of us in the State Department at the time. One person's dream is almost invariably another's nightmare.

Regardless of where you work, dealing with your East is all about cooperation, compromise, and conflict. It is a never-ending game, with many players and few rules or arbiters. Ralph Neas, the executive director for years of the Leadership Conference on Civil Rights, and a man who keeps on his desk the words "Nothing is so full of victory as patience," estimates that he spent some 95 percent of his time working with his East, trying to maintain the cohesion of his coalition:

> As difficult as it is to get a consensus initially on a legislative measure or on a nomination, by far the most challenging part of directing a coalition is maintaining the consensus during the legislative process, because the legislative process always involves compromise. Indeed, no legislation can go through Congress without compromise. And of course, when the circumstances dictate a timely compromise, then you always have the delicate balancing act of trying to help fashion an agreement that will secure you the needed congressional votes without compromising core principles. If this goal is not accomplished to everyone's satisfaction, then certain parts of the coalition may denounce the compromise as a "sellout," and all that we worked so hard for may fall apart.

George Kenney worked on the Yugoslav desk in the State Department before he resigned in 1992. During his tenure, a large part of his day was consumed with writing and, more important, clearing with colleagues and superiors the draft statements and responses to anticipated questions to be used by Margaret Tutwiler, then the State Department's spokesperson, in her daily media briefings. His description of a typical morning's exertion illustrates how much time and effort even relatively simple tasks can require:

> I would come in between about 6 and 6:30 in the morning. I would go up to INR [the Bureau of Intelligence and Research] and I would read the special traffic [intelligence cables]; I also had a friend in INR who would do a pull of wire service stories for me. So I'd get that every day. Then I'd go down to the office and I'd look over the regular traffic and also two or three newspapers: the *New York Times*, the *Washington Post*, maybe the *Wall Street Journal*, maybe the *Financial Times*. Sometimes, by around 7:30, 7:45, I'd call our embassy in Belgrade and talk to one of the staff for half an hour or forty minutes. . . . If I had other questions about what was going on, I might call INR or the CIA or somebody else to double check facts. By about 8 or so, I'd get questions from Margaret through the European Bureau's press office. . . I'd write until about 9:30. . . Margaret needed it by 11:00. From 9:30 to 10:30 I'd take it around for clearances—involving anywhere from four or five people up to ten or twelve. At 10:30 it would go to the front office. I would get six or ten inputs so I'd arbitrate. . . . It got to the point where I asked the European Bureau administrative office if I could have a multiline phone; I explained why and they gave me one.

It would be wrong, however, to view your East as little more than a time-consuming obstacle. Interaction with colleagues can often prompt new ideas and new considerations; even a hallway chat can provide useful information or perspective. (A friend once defined "conversation" as an "opportunity to pick somebody's brain clean.") Colleagues also provide a testing ground for your ideas. It is almost always better to try out a new thought on your East rather than your West, where the costs can be higher when ideas and proposals are shot down. So think of your East as not only necessary but also useful.

Seven Rules for Dealing with Colleagues

There is no way to eliminate the competition inherent in dealings with your East, but it is possible to keep it to a minimum and to increase the chances for productive interaction. Here are some rules that will serve you well.

Work hard on establishing personal relationships. This is what I call the George Bush rule. You never know when the day will come that you need someone. Make it your goal to know as many people to your East as possible—and as well as possible. It is critical to have a reservoir of trust to draw upon. Bush explains why. "If you know somebody, you develop a mutual trust. They're not going to change their government's policy to accommodate you, but you're less apt to have misunderstandings. And you're more apt to get agreement." Many people made fun of Bush's "dial diplomacy," but his phone calls and all that staying in touch came in handy after Saddam Hussein invaded Kuwait and Bush had to cobble together the international coalition that eventually prevailed.

Do not get hung up on rank or protocol. Go to the people who know the issues best and who have a reputation for getting things done. They may be at your level, below, or above—it matters not. Seek out talent and associate yourself with it.

Resist the temptation to include in any meeting or decisionmaking process only those inclined to agree with your views. I say this not out of some sense of morality or legality, but out of self-interest. Inclusion creates the opportunity for a better product, since even those who disagree with you might have something useful to contribute. New ideas may surface; familiar ones may get improved. Those to your East who have a different point of view may save you from greater problems with your West. In addition, including people increases the chance that they will understand what you are trying to do and thus be better able to help you do it. Inclusion becomes critical if the implementation of a decision will fall mostly to the affected party. Also, inclusion makes it less likely that people will go out and work against a policy they opposed. It is far easier to gain compliance if people believe they have had a chance to affect the decision and that their interests received adequate consideration. All of us want to be treated fairly, and most of us react badly when we are not.

Control as much of the policymaking process as possible. The person who calls the meetings, decides on those attending, oversees the preparation of background materials, puts together the agenda, chairs the meeting, monitors the follow-through, and drafts the speech or announcement has the upper hand. You will enjoy greater influence if you draft a policy document and are the person taking comments from others and circulating redrafts, even though it takes more time.

There is an exception to this rule. It only makes sense to be in control if the project is high on your agenda. A good deal of what goes on in any organization is secondary, but everything takes time. There is an opportunity cost: while you are doing one thing, you are not doing something else. You have to ask yourself constantly whether the development of a given policy is the best use of your time. If not, delegate it or let one of your colleagues run with it.

Study your colleagues. Few of us have the insights and skills of a consummate politician such as FDR—"He knew how to persuade one person by argument, another by charm, another by a display of self-confidence, another by flattery, another by encyclopedic knowledge"[2]—but all of us can do better at learning about our colleagues and how best to approach them.

Be willing to share credit. This is easier advocated than done, possibly because those in the public sector normally must content themselves with intangible rewards. Walter Plosila has this to say:

> You need to get others to own things and be part of what it is you are trying to do and learn how to delegate to them significant roles to play. One of the things I found most frustrating about the public sector is they worry so much about who gets credit. It's unbelievable how much pettiness goes on in the public sector at all levels. . . . You can still get credit

by sharing. Sharing credit doesn't mean you don't get any credit. There's this assumption that there's this zero sum on credit. There isn't.

Be a person of your word. Richard Armitage is again worth listening to:

> Both in government and in the private sector you need to deliver on your word. In government, I think this is often overlooked—[some think] you don't need to deliver because there is no bottom line so to speak—but I found that there is a need to deliver, because if you are going to be seen as competent in government, you have to have credibility. And the only way you are going to have credibility with your colleagues in government, which is an absolute key, is by delivering— whether you deliver your boss if you are an underling, or whether you deliver on a commitment.

Turf Wars

Even if you follow all these rules, confrontation, even conflict, will characterize some of your dealings with your East. It is not always pleasant. Often the most bitter and prolonged battles have little to do with issues, but a great deal to do with turf. Conflicts over turf are about who gets to control (or, more often, vie for control) over a certain issue or realm. At times you will be on the defensive, trying to protect what you see as your turf; at other times, the roles will be reversed, and you will be playing offense, trying to get the chance to affect a policy.

It is easiest to play defense when you are the line authority, the person who has the authority to act. When this is the case, you need to ask yourself whether your own interests are served by excluding others from the decisionmaking process. Do those to your East have anything constructive to offer that might improve the quality of the decision or affect its prospects for implementation?

Do you need their help on another issue—possibly one you want to get involved in? Is there a deal to be made? If the answers to these and similar questions are yes, let them in.

If the answer is no—if they have nothing constructive to offer, no legitimate grounds for inclusion, and will simply complicate matters by increasing the number of signatures required to move ahead or heightening the chance of leaks—then keeping them out and protecting your turf is probably a good idea. But make sure the issue is sufficiently important to you before you spend time and effort building a fence around it. And when the stakes are high, check first with your staff and your boss to make sure they agree and will back you up.

Similarly, you need to think through the pros and cons before trying to accumulate turf or gain access to someone else's. Be certain you have a legitimate reason to be involved in an issue; it helps if you can show how the issue affects or is affected by something for which you are responsible. Instead of a frontal attack, try asking to be allowed in or angling for an invitation. Informal hints by your staff to somebody else's staff can help; so too can enlisting as allies others to your East. If these efforts fail, you can seek assistance from your boss, but his or her help is more likely to be forthcoming when you can point to some policy failure and show that a better decision would have been made (or a particular agenda advanced) if only you had been included from the start.

At times, your turf will overlap with someone else's, and you will have to decide whether to play offense, defense, or even both. Ron Brown, President Clinton's secretary of commerce, was one of several cabinet-level officers involved in U.S. trade policy. Historically trade issues have sparked a good deal of internecine struggle, as they do in the current administration. In an effort to diminish the infighting, Brown held frequent conversations with his counterparts; he also chose a mix of offensive and defensive strategies that reflected his agenda and his bureaucratic strengths and weaknesses:

> You carve out specific areas where first of all you want to make a personal commitment, because they're interesting

and exciting to you and you think they make a difference. You carve out areas that you've got some right to, some claim on, that probably supersedes the claims of others with forks in the pot. So you don't starve. You're not trying to claw your way up. And you carve out things that you really think make a difference to the administration. . . . You keep your oar in the water on some [other] things, but you pick out a couple of things where you ought to be preeminent.

Once again, the key is to retain your focus. Avoid distractions. Do not get involved in turf wars for their own sake. They should only be a last resort, and then only if you are fighting over a critical element of your agenda. Resist the temptation to poach, and be generous unless it really would be counterproductive. Richard Perle argues for discipline in resisting the seductions of turf wars:

A lot of people spend a lot of time and get into a lot of difficulty in the executive branch because they want more and more responsibility. They want other people's responsibility. They can't bear the idea that anybody else has responsibility so they are constantly reaching out and grabbing. That never appealed to me. I was interested in shedding responsibility. There were subjects that bored me and that I did not think were terribly important. I was delighted to have other people deal with them. I never wanted to hear about them. More often than not, the people who worked for me would say, "Look, you've got to listen to this. I've got to tell you what's going on with the Spanish." Well, I didn't give a damn what was going on with them. I didn't like the Spanish. I didn't think the Spanish had anything to contribute to Western defense. And I didn't want to hear about the Spanish. And I certainly didn't want to take jurisdiction away from somebody down the hall. So I saved myself a lot of time.

Shared authorities all but guarantee friction, and in the world of politics and the public sector, almost all authority is shared. At a minimum, your goal should be to keep the friction under control, to avoid unnecessary fights, and to develop a mechanism for resolving differences. More positively, a constructive relationship with key players to your East can contribute to your other relationships and add measurably to your overall effectiveness and to the prospects for realizing your agenda.

Meetings

Most often, interaction with colleagues takes place at meetings, always important arenas in institutional life. We have already looked at staff meetings from the perspectives of both the boss and the subordinate; meetings with colleagues, though, are entirely different. Here you must follow one binding rule: do not attend a meeting unless you have determined what you want to accomplish and what you need to do to accomplish it. "Be prepared" should be your motto.

Being prepared entails more than you think. Your first decision is whether to call for a meeting, attend a meeting someone else has called, or send someone in your place. You only want to call for a meeting—which immediately establishes you as de facto chairman—if it serves your goals. The purpose of a meeting can be substantive (you have identified an issue that needs to be addressed) or procedural (you have decided to impose some discipline on the policy process). You can use a meeting to stymie something, to stop it from happening. Meetings can also be a place to trade information, to ensure that the left hand knows what the right is doing. A productive meeting can resolve an issue. A poorly handled meeting can accomplish just the opposite. Meetings can distract people, while the real work happens elsewhere—which may be part of your plan.

Obviously, there are a lot of angles to consider. Whom should you invite? In principle, you should invite anyone who has a legitimate stake in the meeting's subject matter. You do not want anyone there who is superfluous; such people tend to clutter up the conversation, increase the chance of leaks, and inhibit those in the know from speaking up. But you do not want to leave out any-one who has a good reason to be there. First of all, it will be hard to justify if that person calls you or if his or her boss bothers yours. Second, people are more likely to make trouble for you, either by leaking or frustrating implementation, if they are not included. Third, you forfeit the opportunity to persuade someone—or to be persuaded. Arguments and facts can change minds, and meetings provide an arena for airing out facts and arguments, sometimes to good effect.

Beforehand, prepare and circulate an agenda and background papers. This can help reduce the amount of time wasted and increase the odds that those who attend are well enough informed to contribute something useful. If you know the meeting may cause controversy, get in touch hours or even days ahead. One of my former colleagues in government avoided simply confronting people with a position paper (on the grounds that they would be put off by something so formal) unless she had first told them what was coming and explained her motivation.

Look to both your North and South before heading East. If your boss has a stake in the outcome of the meeting, you should check to make sure that you are on the same wave length. You may also want to sit down with your staff, who sometimes know more about the detail of an issue than you do. Always read any relevant material and ask questions of your staff and others. There is no substitute for making the time and effort to master the subject matter.

Mastery is important, but it is not enough. You should also think through what others might want to accomplish. You may be able to align yourself with one or more of them, letting them do the hard work for you. This can be especially useful if you are pre-pared to come away with half a loaf; you can then act as the rea-sonable person of compromise, putting forth your bridging pro-posal at the point of an apparent impasse.

It is easier to position yourself for such a maneuver—or, indeed, for any objective—if you do some intelligence gathering ahead of time. A useful comparison comes from the world of sports, where teams "scout" or collect information about their opponents before a game. I am not suggesting that you cheat or spy, but a few phone calls from you or your staff may turn up surprising information. A conversation or a meeting between you and another central person before the meeting might prove useful in your gaining a better understanding of all that is at stake.

An instructive example of poor preparation for a meeting comes from a cabinet meeting I attended during the Gulf crisis in early 1991. (Only members of the cabinet get to sit in the high chairs around the table in the cabinet room, but a few staff members such as myself could sometimes get in and sit on one of the chairs that hug the walls.) The meeting was held to brief the cabinet (many of whom would then have to brief their own staffs and the press) on the upcoming State of the Union address. President Bush had the chief of staff, John Sununu, quickly describe the contents of the speech, much of which focused on foreign policy. Bush then asked for any questions or comments in a manner that suggested he really did not want any. Nonetheless, Jack Kemp, the secretary of housing and urban development, spoke up. He argued for including something more on domestic issues, in particular a call for "empowerment" and the development of programs that would give individuals and communities greater control over resources and their own lives.

The quality of Kemp's proposals is not the issue here; the fact is, they never had a chance. An awkward silence greeted his remarks, followed by a barrage of criticism. Since he had not prepared the ground for his own intervention, no one was forthcoming with support.

What might Kemp have done? Days before the meeting, he could have lined up some of those around the table known to be sympathetic to his views and equally unhappy with the draft speech to speak out in favor of his proposal. He could then have come to the meeting with specific language to add to the draft speech. It might have been too late; even so, had he done so, he would not have been isolated in the meeting or speaking into a void. His lack of preparation cost him: his comment was ignored and strained his already uneasy relations with several of his colleagues.[3]

Chairing Meetings

Meetings have a bad reputation, and often for good reason. But they need not be a waste of time; on the contrary, meetings can actually save time (and increase efficiency) if they are conducted well. But chairing meetings is an art form. There are essentially three styles, only two of which I recommend. I will call them assertive, tight, and loose. A loose chairman will allow a lot of general conversation and not object when people deviate from the agenda or talk at length. While some of this can be useful to break the ice, it can be terribly inefficient. I much prefer the tight chairman, who knows in advance just how much time he will devote to each agenda item and will keep things moving along, or an assertive chairman, who suggests a decision at the outset in order to force people to take a stand,

My former colleague Robert Gates was an assertive as well as tight chairman. He convened many meetings of a subcabinet-level management committee—a six-person committee dubbed "the small group" for reasons that had nothing to do with the egos around the table—during the 1990–91 Gulf crisis. Gates ran a tight meeting, and he would often begin discussion of a controversial issue with his preferred outcome. This approach was also preferred but carried to an extreme by Margaret Thatcher, who was described to me as someone who "would come into a meeting, sit down, announce what the conclusions were as far as she was concerned, and then look defiantly around the table and challenge anyone to fight her about them." This method runs the risk of prejudicing the outcome—although the risk is limited if the people at the meeting are essentially of the same rank—but it has the great advantage of cutting quickly to the heart of the matter and getting people down to details. It allows you to accomplish a lot and, better yet, to accomplish it quickly.

If you are chairing a meeting, you have special responsibilities. It is up to the chair to see that due process is followed. This includes inviting those who need or deserve to be there, circulating an agenda, and making sure that necessary background materials are provided in advance so that people can read them and not waste time getting briefed at the meeting. It is also a good idea to warn people in advance if you intend to call on them for a special presentation. At the meeting, it is up to you to see that the agenda is followed and that everyone gets a sufficient chance to air his or her views.

The most important work often comes at the end of the meeting. It is always a good idea to summarize what was decided and what follow-up is to be done by whom and by when. Assume nothing; actually, assume the worst. The Japanese film *Rashomon* is instructive here. This classic remake of Shakespeare's *Macbeth* shows how perception colors what people experience. No two people see or recall the same event exactly the same way; no two people at your meeting will walk away with the same recollection of what was decided and who has what responsibility. Sometimes it is as if they were at different meetings. So sum up and be specific, if need be following up the meeting by distributing minutes or, better yet, with a record of decisions and responsibilities.

You can go a long way if you can run a decent meeting. Remember, chairing a meeting with colleagues is very different from chairing a meeting of your staff. Within limits, you can direct the latter, but persuasion is your only tool with those of relatively equal rank. Your persuasiveness with your East can be enhanced by the knowledge that behind your words and actions lies power—either your own or that of your boss. But such power should be used sparingly, for it is quickly used up, and its frequent use can inspire a rebellion. With colleagues it is normally better to think of yourself as guiding the meeting rather than running it.

Ground Rules for Negotiating

Meetings are only one form of interaction with your East. A good part of your day will be spent dealing with your counterparts from your own and other organizations. Much of this interaction will be a kind of negotiation. We normally think of negotiating as something more formal, done by diplomats or lawyers. Yet most of what we do, however informal or even casual, involves some negotiating. As Richard Neustadt has pointed out, "The power to persuade is the power to bargain."[4] It is extremely rare that you and your colleagues will agree on all facets of an issue, from the decision itself to how it should be implemented. Some disagreement, whether on basics or peripherals, is all but inevitable.

Ultimate agreement is often possible; ideally, you can help negotiate an agreement in which everyone walks away satisfied that, even though they did not get all that they wanted, they are better off with the deal than without it. This is the classic "win-win" scenario. Unfortunately, it is not always within reach. Some issues do not lend themselves to compromise; even if some issues do, some people do not. As a result, negotiations can become "zero-sum"—one person or faction gains at the expense of another. And in extreme cases, negotiations can come to naught, as the parties are unable or unwilling to agree to any sort of compromise. In these circumstances, it is usually best to cut your losses and not waste time working on the impossible. Either put the issue aside for a while, or refer it to your North for a decision or to your South for further consideration.

Numerous books have been written about negotiating techniques, about how to resolve differences, about how to maximize your own objectives, about how to get *to* yes or *past* no.[5] As the best of these books acknowledge, there are few if any universal rules about negotiating tactics. One of the most talented and successful negotiators I have ever known, former UN official Giandomenico Picco, says flatly that "technique is always ancillary to ideas," and that if anything else matters, it is "individual credibility." Specific approaches need to be tailored for the specific situation—the stakes, your own depth of commitment, the positions of others involved, the bias and disposition of the decisionmaker, and so on. What follows are some points to keep in mind when negotiating—points consistent with more general guidelines for how best to deal with your East, points that will also come in handy when negotiating with others:

Expect to negotiate. Disagreements with colleagues are inevitable. Some you will be able to solve; some you should solve when the differences are small and the stakes do not warrant bucking it up to a more senior level. Making a sincere effort to resolve differences is never a waste of time. Make sure differences are worth disagreeing about. Keep in mind the adage attributed to the seventeenth-century Spanish philosopher Baltasar Gracián, "Don't take the wrong side of an argument just because your opponent has taken the right side."[6] Former congressman and secretary of defense Les Aspin reportedly asked himself three questions before getting into a scrape: "One, what is the fight really about? Two, who will win and who will lose? Three, what are the true implications?" In short, before you put on the gloves, make sure the immediate stakes justify getting into a fight, that you have a shot at winning, and that the likely benefits of fighting over this issue justify the costs to your relationships with your colleagues.[7]

Do not fall into the NIH trap. NIH has nothing to do with the National Institutes of Health; rather, it stands for "not invented here." Do not disagree just because somebody else has an idea and he or she will garner the credit. Moreover, if the idea is yours, and you sense that someone else is suffering from the NIH affliction, you may want to share the glory in order to get the idea adopted and implemented. As the old saw goes, there is no limit to what you can accomplish if you don't care who gets the credit. John Lewis, the former civil rights leader turned congressman, makes this point with passion:

> It's always seemed to me that the people who are fed by and who focus on visibility and notoriety and getting the credit don't have what you might call staying power. They rise and

fall in the public eye, here today and gone tomorrow. Too often they become flashes in the pan, winding up in those "Where Are They Now?" columns. It's sad. Dr. King used to talk about this. He said individuals who fall in love with public attention are not worthy of it. People who hunger for fame don't realize that if they're in the spotlight today, somebody else will be tomorrow. Fame never lasts. The work you do, the things you accomplish—that's what endures. That's what really means something.[8]

Outprepare the other guy. Before you enter into any negotiation, know your facts. You can have a great deal of influence over the thinking and behavior of others if you know more about the issues at hand than they do. As usual, there is no substitute for homework.

Determine in advance your own bottom line. Rarely will others simply give you all that you desire. Decide in advance what is the minimum you are prepared to accept (or the maximum you are prepared to give up). Think through what is central to your concerns and what is secondary or even peripheral. Ask yourself beforehand what probable price you will have to pay to win over a key player and decide whether you are willing and able to pay it.

BATNA

Figure out what your boss wants and what latitude you have. In some cases this may mean checking before a meeting or conversation. You never want to get into the situation where your handling of a negotiation leaves you vulnerable to accusations that you gave away the farm; nor do you want to invest a lot in holding the line only to be undermined by your boss, who may care much less about a certain position than you do.

Fight hard if it matters and if you have backing. If a key issue on your agenda is on the table, and if you know you have backing or can get it, be prepared to fight long and hard. Ross Sandler, someone who did a good deal of fighting when he was New York City's transportation commissioner, articulates this point well:

> The most important thing from the public perspective was to understand what your primary objectives were and to go after

them, and not be afraid. And to attack your enemies in government. These are not personal enemies, but institutional enemies. The only person who has a stake in the success of a line manager is that line manager. Personnel? They're much more interested in comparability of salaries and in reducing the number of job titles. . . . If you want to win these battles, you've got to do it in a way that makes them want to support you. They're not going to support you out of the goodness of their heart. Leasing? Every agency has space needs. They take them in order. Why should they take you out of order? Because you have a crisis? They don't care. OMB? They've got to balance the budget. They've got to take care of a thousand requests. You're just another request. Don't worry whether you're popular. There are some things you can negotiate. You negotiate those. There are certain things you can't negotiate. And those you have to appeal right up the ladder. And the ones who don't appeal are taking risks for the public and for themselves. . . . The people who make tremendous differences in these agencies are those who have decided they are going to fight the battles that have to be fought while they're there.

Learn as much as you can about the positions of the others involved. Often, what happens before the formal meeting or negotiating session is more important than the negotiations themselves. Learn all you can about your colleagues—who can be coopted, who can be won over, who must be resisted and if need be defeated, who has real authority and who does not. Court your colleagues; there may be an opportunity to work out a common position with several important people, thereby allowing you to get the core of what you want. Alternatively, you may learn that others are likely to espouse opposing views. This opens up the middle ground, and you can enter as the great compromiser.

Learn as much as possible about the negotiating style of others. Except in those rare instances in which you develop relations with individuals to your East that allow you to dispense with almost all preliminaries and posturing, you will find it difficult to escape the need to negotiate. With some people, there is no chance of agreement unless you are prepared to accede to their terms. Fortunately, most people are more flexible, but they will need to bargain before they can agree to anything; with them, it is best to start high and compromise. They will be able to return to their boss and staff and point to what they gained; you will be able to return to your boss and staff and point to what you got. Sir Harold Nicolson divides people into two sorts: the "warrior or heroic" and the "mercantile or shop-keeper." He writes: "The former regards diplomacy as 'war by other means'; the latter regards it as an aid to peaceful commerce."[9] Negotiation with warriors tends to be confrontational and winner-take-all; make sure you are up to it and, if the stakes necessitate, consider using this approach yourself. Negotiation with shopkeepers, on the other hand, almost always ends in a deal; in these situations, ask yourself if a deal is worth having.

Do not be bullied or stampeded. Expect to be tested and pressured; those across the table will be looking for weaknesses in you and your case, just as you will be looking for weaknesses in their position. People will drop names and suggest all sorts of possible consequences if you do not come around. Take these with a grain of salt. When I was a junior Pentagon official, I recall telling my boss, Admiral Daniel Murphy, that the White House wanted something of us. Murphy smiled and told me about the time years before when he was military assistant to Secretary of Defense Melvin Laird. Murphy came rushing in to Laird's office, saying the White House was on the phone wanting an answer to a question. Laird told Murphy to calm himself, reminded him that the White House was a building and buildings cannot place phone calls, and said that when the president phoned and asked him directly (and not someone using the president's name) he would respond. Murphy duly reported this to his counterpart across the Potomac; "the White House" backed off.

Do not ask for the impossible. Part of learning about those around the table is knowing the extent of their brief. It makes no sense to demand something you know they do not have the power to accept unless you do not want to reach agreement for one reason or another. Robert Strauss tells this story about the time he was chief trade negotiator for the United States:

> The first thing I did was say to the Europeans, "We have no intention of destroying the Common Agricultural Policy. I'd love to make you give it up. It's a terrible policy. I know you would like to get rid of it. But I know you can't do it politically, and so there is no point in my demanding it. So I give you my word we will not demand the end of the Common Agricultural Policy, as bad as it is, as much as you might like to get rid of it, because you concluded that the farmers in France will destroy you." What I wanted was to get our nose further under the tent, begin the process, so that twenty or thirty years from now someone will be able to deal with it . . . once they were convinced of that, they were ready to line up and help us squeeze the Japanese and be brought along on the deal. You need to find out what the other side can live with and can't live with. Go as far as you can, get as much as you can, but there's no point in demanding something they can't give.

Help your opposite number and help yourself. Remember that you are not the only person at the table who has a compass and a set of relationships to manage. Part of knowing your opponent is knowing his situation and what he needs to make an agreement stick. It does no good to strike a deal only to see it blow up when the others return home. One experienced U.S. diplomat explains the importance of viewing your opposite number as a partner, not just an adversary:

> One of the main things I learned about negotiations is knowing the scope of your opponent's latitude. And in government it is really understanding his political constraints. I think that is perhaps as important as anything else in negotiations . . . trying to craft proposals in a way that would give

your negotiating partner the opportunity to sell it at home. . . . If you get [something] that was acceptable to you, you don't waste time saying I might have gotten 10 per cent more. In government, you normally negotiate in a public context, and it is important that you start above where you are willing to finish so your opponent can say he got you down.

Sir Robin Renwick, a former British ambassador to South Africa, played a major role in helping to free Nelson Mandela from prison. One key to Renwick's effectiveness was his government's willingness to offer limited incentives to the South African government that were conditional on its taking partial steps toward the ultimate goal of ending apartheid. In this way, the British maintained pressure but also made it easier on South Africa's minority government to justify any compromise—in this case, the release of Mandela—to its own core constituency. Renwick describes his strategy:

> We told the South African Government before they released Mandela, that if they did release Mandela, we would respond. We did not say, "No, you must do everything immediately, until there is one person, one vote, we will not respond," [rather], we said, "We are going to respond immediately by lifting the ban on new investments in South Africa and if you then take the next step and unban the ANC [African National Congress] and the Communist party, we will respond to that. Each step you take will meet with a response from us."

Do not cave in to pressure to reach an agreement. No agreement can be better than a bad one, so always ask yourself a number of questions before signing on to compromises that make agreement possible. Are you are better off with or without this agreement? If the issue gets referred to another level, are you more likely to get the outcome you want? How will your boss react? How will refusing to compromise beyond a certain point affect your other interests and relationships at every point on your compass? Is continuing to negotiate worth the time and effort, or would you be better off devoting yourself to another issue more ripe for resolution? There is a pressure to compromise that sometimes needs to be resisted. If necessary, be obstinate. The search for consensus can be a trap. It can reduce results to a lowest common denominator that is less than you require—and less than you can get if you hold out or appeal. Indeed, the willingness to leave the table without an agreement can give you the leverage to get what you want.

Never distort information. Never withhold what others to your East have a legitimate right to know. Your credibility is always at stake in a negotiation, and you stand to lose a great deal more than what is on the table if you sully your reputation for honesty.

Beware of bluffing. Before you bluff, make sure you are willing to suffer the consequences of having your bluff called.

Never lose your cool except when you choose to. Losing self-control will not help you think more clearly, will not make it easier to get your way, and will not make it easier to get along with your colleagues on the next issue. The exception is when you have determined that a display of temper might help you get what you want—if not on the issue at hand, then perhaps down the road.

It may make sense to change the mix. If there is deadlock and you want the dispute resolved (because there is no higher level to move it up to or you fear your purposes will not be served by the issue's being moved up to your North), is there anything you can add to the mix of what is being considered to change the calculations of others? Richard Nixon is cited as believing that one way to resolve impasses on narrow issues is "by raising the level to a comprehensive approach so that dickering can take place along a broad front."[10] Sometimes you can break an impasse by expanding what is on the table. It may seem counter-intuitive, but sometimes a negotiation gets simpler by becoming more complex. This is what the Bush administration did in the Middle East in 1991: by introducing multiple tracks for negotiations, we made it possible for parties to trade off compensation in one area for what they could not get in another.

Look out for those who say yes but mean no. Often, those who agree to a point with conditions (the so-called "yes, but" position) are in effect saying no. George Shultz describes this as "a standard Pentagon tactic: when you don't want to do something, agree to do it—but with such an impossible set of conditions and on such a preposterously gigantic scale that the outcome will be to do nothing."[11] If you are tempted to use this technique, do so only if you are prepared to take yes for an answer. In the wake of Iraq's invasion of Kuwait, military leaders told President Bush that responding could require hundreds of thousands of soldiers; Bush took them at their word and told them to deploy whatever troops and equipment they needed. The rest is history.

Be careful about agreements in principle. At some point, someone will try to get you to agree to a framework document or to some other form of "agreement in principle," with the specifics to be "worked out" over time, whether by you and your counterpart or by your staff members. Remember, the devil as well as God can be in the details. Never satisfy yourself with an "in principle, yes" until you have heard all of the conditions that must be met before principle becomes practice. The danger is that you will think you have achieved more than you really have and, once having advertised your "accomplishment," you will find yourself pressured to agree on second-order issues that in fact are of primary consequence.

Know the pros and cons of negotiating publicly and privately. In private, it is easier to explore new mixes, to broker compromises, to walk away from positions, even to abandon the negotiations altogether. It is thus not surprising that secret negotiations in Oslo between Israelis and Palestinians succeeded when visible diplomacy appeared stalemated. In general, once the fact of negotiations becomes known, and especially once positions become public, any compromise may be perceived as a sign of weakness, making it more difficult to gain political support for whatever emerges. At the same time, publicity can also strengthen your hand, for you can claim credibly to your interlocutor that compromise on your part is not sustainable and that he must give way—something that may be difficult for him for similar reasons. Negotiations conducted in public therefore tend to be more difficult to bring to closure. Woodrow Wilson's pledge—"open covenants openly arrived at"—can prevent the arrival of any covenants at all. Unless this is your goal, privacy is usually the best course.

Remember that deadlines can be dangerous. Deadlines are fine if they promote closure when the differences are small or if they lead automatically to consideration of issues at a higher level. But deadlines can also create pressure for compromise and agreement when you might be better off without one. Think twice before suggesting or agreeing to any kind of time frame.

Examine carefully the motives of those asking for more time. Often, those advocating delay—whether to gain more time for review or to hear from others not there—are stalling to avoid coming to a decision where they fear they would not prevail. Some requests for postponing a decision are reasonable, but past the point of reason, delay becomes tantamount to a no. Bring the issue to closure at this point, if need be without consensus. If you are in a position to make a decision despite a lack of consensus, let the decision move forward with dissent noted.

Beware the "slippery slope" argument. Some negotiators will argue that any compromise, no matter how small, creates precedents and pressures for unacceptable compromise; this stance often makes reaching an agreement impossible. When you encounter it, it is usually best to step away from the table. Try to find another forum for decision, or even work behind the scenes to change the instructions given to your adversary. But do not expect the current negotiation to bear fruit.

Disagree without declaring war. In government and other organizations, you invariably have to work with the same people on a range of issues. Be careful not to allow bitterness or anger promoted by one issue to spill over and affect other concerns. Wess Roberts, the author of several popular books on management, offers a useful maxim: "Do not consider all opponents to be enemies."[12] Former Massachusetts governor William Weld tells the following story about resisting the temptation to escalate political disagreement:

> You've got to keep it away from the personal and on the issues. For example, the Speaker [of the Massachusetts House of Representatives] very much opposed educational reform for teachers and the educational reform bill that the Senate President and I both wanted with respect to expanding school choice. . . . The Speaker won. The House wouldn't budge. The teacher's lobby is very strong in the House. Somebody else might have impugned the Speaker's motives, and said that he was beholden to the teacher's lobby. But it's just possible that he felt that the changes would undermine public education. Which was what he said to me privately and publicly. I couldn't prove he was wrong. So what's the percentage in impugning his motives?

The answer, of course, is "none." Keep the debate centered on the issues; bringing personality into it will not help you resolve this disagreement and will only make it harder to resolve future ones. The East is a permanent and central part of your political environment, and effectiveness demands that you act with restraint and perspective.

Conclusions

The East represents the essence of politics, and working effectively with those to your East requires an appreciation of the distribution of power. You cannot do much by yourself; a key to success in political life is persuading others to do what you consider the right thing. If you focus on persuading others to adopt your goals, you will have accomplished a great deal.

Much of your life in any organization will be spent negotiating in one way or another with colleagues, often in meetings. Know in advance what you must protect and what you can compromise. Avoid unnecessary battles—especially over turf—and avoid fighting any battle harder than the stakes warrant. Remember, your aim is not to defeat people or to enlarge your area of responsibility, but to realize your agenda.

Your ability to succeed with your colleagues, with your East, will depend in part on your success in dealing with your North and South. Colleagues will have no choice but to take you seriously if it is known that you have a close relationship with your boss, that you reflect your boss's views and will be backed up accordingly. Similarly, your own staff members—both by how they prepare you and by how they themselves deal with their colleagues to their East—will affect your ability to influence your colleagues.

The connections also work in the opposite direction. Your ability to get things done effectively with your East will increase your value to your boss. Similarly, your staff will work harder if its members see that their labors have real impact. What you do in any direction, how you manage every set of relationships, will affect and be affected by what you do in the others.

6

West: Those with Whom You Should Work

AS DIFFICULT AS RELATIONS with North, South, and East—bosses, subordinates, and colleagues—can be, they involve fellow insiders. Usually there exists a common understanding of purpose, realities, and limitations among you.

This commonality of perspectives does not necessarily apply to the fourth and last set of relationships on the compass. Those to your West include all the people and organizations and agencies that affect your ability to succeed—the media, legislatures, interest groups, regulatory agencies, courts, and so on—but are largely if not entirely independent of you. This is not an argument for avoiding them; on the contrary, their power and independence argue for engaging them. Indeed, if your East constitutes those with whom you work—with whom you often *must* work—your West involves those with whom you *should* work.

Why Your West Matters

When I taught at the Kennedy School, the individuals, groups, and institutions to my West were designated "the authorizing environment." It is an awful phrase, for (jargon aside) it connotes a passive, reactive attitude that is unfortunate and even misleading. But it also contains some truth, for your authority often stems from people on the outside who are prepared to support you and in some cases follow your lead (or at least not get in the way).

A better phrase for the West might simply be the external environment. In my last government job, my West included Congress, the media, academic experts, a range of domestic and international special interest groups, foreign governments (both in their capitals and in Washington, through their embassies), and international institutions, such as the United Nations and the World Bank. For most people, the West constitutes the most vexing direction of their compass. It is crucial, though, that you not be put off by this complexity; you should spend adequate time with those to your West. The political scientist James Q. Wilson eloquently makes this point about the need to engage the West:

> The principal source of power is a constituency. This plain fact repeated by generations of students of public administration still seems lost on those people (business executives, in particular) who upon taking a high-level job in Washington complain about the amount of time they must spend attending to the demands and needs of outside groups. All this time spent currying favor and placating critics, they argue, is time taken away from the real work of the agency, which is to "do the job." No. The real work of the agency *is* to curry favor and placate critics.[1]

The importance of paying attention to external constituencies may seem obvious, but it is tempting to do just the opposite. Those who operate outside your organization are often difficult and demanding; few of us volunteer for confrontational encounters that promise to be unsuccessful. Also, the demands of those to your North, South, and East—not to mention your family's needs and your own—tend to come first. It is nearly impossible to say no to your boss, unwise to ignore your subordinates, and difficult to avoid your colleagues, all of whom are part of your daily flow. The fact that those to your West are less likely to cross your path only strengthens the tendency to give them short shrift.

Avoid this temptation at all costs. If you ignore your West, sooner or later you will find yourself stymied, or worse. Just as important, you may be denying yourself a potential ally. If those on the outside can help break you, they also can help make you. The choice is partly yours. Paul Grogan, former president of the Local Initiatives Support Corporation (LISC), a nonprofit organization devoted to community development, makes the case for seeing—and seizing—your West as an opportunity:

> You can move the political ground. One of the things that distresses me most about people in government is they accept the current political reality as a given. Sort of the fallacy of straight-line projection. This is the way it's going to be, as opposed to moving the political ground. Change the environment so that this issue will be treated differently. If you see that as an objective, you can get room to do things that don't seem to be possible. That's on issues large and small, whether how a city councilor conceives of his control over this or that or changing the whole environment in which a foreign policy decision gets made. You've really got to believe you can change the political ground.

Engaging your West is not easy. It takes a concerted effort. Here is what the former British ambassador to the United States, Robin Renwick, told his young officers at Britain's Washington embassy:

> The pep talk I give them is that it is absolutely useless in this city sitting in your office. You have to go out and see people on the Hill every day, see people in the State Department, the Pentagon, the National Security Council, the White House, the Treasury, every day. And if you don't do that, you will be

taken by surprise. And you have to force yourself to do that. Even though you think you know what's going on, you don't. Things, when they move in this city, move very suddenly. Sometimes we are taken by surprise, but we try to avoid it as far as possible. And that means a positive effort to get off your backsides and out of your office and constantly keeping in touch with key people around the town.

Your West can be an ally. It can compensate for problems with your East and can help you persuade your boss that opportunity (or necessity) knocks. Ross Sandler virtually created his own West in his efforts to build political support for fixing New York City's bridges. He recalls:

A lot of things that government does and needs to do don't necessarily have very strong interest groups. Who speaks for bridges? Who speaks for maintenance of highways? Who says the sewers have got to be repaired? We did a number of things. The first thing we did is we started talking about the problem, and we began bringing the press around. We gave press tours of bridges. We did slide shows, publicly, we talked about what was happening on the bridges. We went to interest groups, from contractors to good-government groups. We were incredibly successful, because it was the first time people began talking about real problems with real information. . . . We generated massive newspaper concern about bridges. We felt we had a crisis on our hands; we knew we were going to have to close bridges, and significant bridges; and so we felt that the only way to deal with that was to be ahead of the curve, to announce it beforehand, and to announce a program beforehand. So this is the problem, this is our solution. You can't just announce problems. You've got to have a solution. And we put together an actual book on bridges—their condition, and what the solutions would be, a whole series of solutions. And we got the mayor to release that as his program and we got the mayor to agree as to what the program should be before we had the largest crisis of a closed bridge. . . . You had to not only do the right thing, you had to let people know you were doing the right thing.

Paul Grogan was, at one time, a city official in Boston under Mayor Kevin White. He, too, enlisted his West to promote inner-city development projects:

As a city official, one dealing with the mayor's political machine and the constraints on public programs, [I tried] to create external constituencies to do what I wanted to do with public programs. . . . In constrained government circum-stances, it is possible to do a kind of "ventriloquism," where there are things you want to do, but if you try to do them all by yourself you are very constrained, but if you get external constituencies who have a voice to say those same things, if you in effect help build or create those constituencies, it allows you to move the government in ways that just were not possible. . . . How do you get a large amount of funds to do something really significant on a very flexible basis to give you this new institution? Well, you mobilize the business com-munity to call for this. It enables the government to do some-thing it normally can't do, which is to make public funding available on a very flexible, seed-capital basis for new and untried institutions and new ideas. It short-circuits the ability of the normal constraints to say "no, you can't do this, this has to be divided up seventeen ways."

But practicing "ventriloquism" and making your West an active ally—or at least preventing it from becoming a major adversary—requires a great deal of work. You never want to simply announce some change in policy; you always want to prepare the way. More important still, never wait until a crisis develops before working with your West. Get to know your West early on, either to head off a crisis or to establish relationships so that if and when a crisis flares up, you will be in a better position to manage it.

You should also avoid the temptation to spend time mostly with your "friends" in your West. It is always nice to be told that you're doing well, and it is important not to take your supporters for granted, but most of your time should be spent with those who are either neutral or even somewhat opposed to you. (On the other hand, dealing with the unalterably opposed is rarely a good use of time, as nothing you can realistically say or do will affect them.) In my last job, I held or attended or addressed scores of meetings with Jewish-American groups precisely because they were uncomfortable with the Bush administration's policies toward the Middle East. I wanted to give them an opportunity to suggest ideas and to vent their frustration over what we were doing; these meetings also gave me a chance to explain our objectives and to temper their anger. It was time spent profitably—if not always enjoyably.

Dealing Effectively with Your West

Ideally, relations with your West should begin during a transition, either to help get you over a confirmation hurdle (if one exists), or, in all cases, to help you develop your agenda and build the support that will be necessary for its implementation. Read what Joseph Fernandez—tapped in 1989 to become the head of New York City's public schools—did in the three months between the time he was named and the day he took office, this while he was still running Miami's school system:

> From September to January, I participated in 162 meetings. I'd come into New York on a Thursday night or a Friday, stay until Sunday night, and in between, at any and all hours, meet with every conceivable member of my new constituency: politicians, business people, union leaders, reporters, editors, councilmen, parent groups, the heads of advocacy groups, arts groups—a long list [Stan] Litow carefully assembled. I met with the outgoing mayor, Ed Koch, and the mayor-to-be David Dinkins. I met with all the editorial boards, some more than once, and all the daily beat reporters. For each group, I outlined my legislative agenda, my budget agenda, and

answered questions. I'd start at seven o'clock in the morning, sometimes with two or three breakfast meetings in a row, and go until late in the evening. It wasn't unusual to make twenty-five meetings on a weekend. If it was scheduled, I was there.[2]

As Fernandez's stormy and abbreviated tenure in New York demonstrates, early consultation will not ensure the cooperation and support of your West. But it will increase the odds of winning support and tend to decrease the intensity of opposition when it arises. People everywhere want to be stroked, to be asked for their opinions and advice, to be wooed. As you get to know those to your West, remember that, as always, little things matter—returning phone calls, being available for meetings, showing up on time, attending cocktail parties, giving speeches at conventions. Your West will demand a lot of time, but it is usually time well spent.

Engaging your West sooner than later is better for several reasons. First, once an issue is cast and the public develops an impression, it can be very hard to shake. Dan Quayle is a case in point: his successful ventures as vice president were offset by the occasional blunder, in large part because his mistakes only confirmed the image that many held of him. A similar phenomenon was at work with Lani Guinier, President Clinton's initial choice to head the Justice Department's civil rights division, who suffered from a sluggish effort by the administration to promote her candidacy, allowing her opponents to define her and her views. The Clinton administration also paid a price for being so slow to articulate a defense of the North American Free Trade Agreement (NAFTA). Although it passed, the struggle was more costly and difficult than it needed to be owing to the time NAFTA's opponents had to shape public perceptions.

Prompt overtures to your West can also be critical if you enter a job with some sort of political baggage. When Ron Brown became chairman of the Democratic National Committee, he was viewed with suspicion by powerful elements of the party because of his close ties to Jesse Jackson. But a primary in Chicago just months after Brown took office gave him an early chance to demonstrate his independence, and he seized it by supporting the party's choice rather than the African-American candidate favored by Jackson. Brown continued working hard at his problem:

> It was really just massive outreach efforts. I spent a lot of time with leadership in the Jewish community, because the Jesse [Jackson] connection made me very suspect even though I'd been close to a lot of the Jewish community organizations for years. People who knew me trusted and respected me, but the word was out, he's a Jesse person. So I spent a lot of time doing those sorts of things. I also spent a good deal of time [with moderates]—one of my first major speeches was to the DLC [Democratic Leadership Council] meeting that year in Philadelphia, spending some time with the more moderate wing of the party.

A third reason to cultivate your West early and often is that it can be the best way to head off problems or even accomplish some good. As Ohio's attorney general, Lee Fisher established a business outreach program to deal with a principal external constituency before it became a problem for him:

> On a regular basis I meet with a varied group of business people, very often people who are Republicans and Independents as opposed to Democrats. . . . The purpose is to explain to them what it is the office of the attorney general does and specifically what it is we do that impacts the business community. I try to explain to them that I do not want the business community to view us as confrontational, but instead to let them know where they can access us to actually prevent a problem from being created. For example, in the environmental area, we explain to businesses that they can seek us out for advice in advance of doing something; or in the antitrust area, they can seek us in advance of our taking an action and we will be glad to give them informal advice. And I often quote to the businessmen what a torts professor

said to me in law school, that "it's better to have a fence at the top of a cliff than to have an ambulance below." Because all too often in government and the law, we're ambulance drivers waiting for someone to get hurt so we can pick up the pieces, whether it's a child who's been abused or hooked on drugs, or waiting for someone to violate the law and send them to jail or impose a fine on the company for polluting the air.

One more reason to engage your West as soon as possible is that once a decision is made or a policy is set in stone, you are essentially confronting people with a take-it-or-leave-it choice. Whether for reasons of pique over not being included, or because you ignored some item central to their agenda, they may choose to oppose you. Talking to Harry Truman regarding foreign aid policy, Senator Arthur Vandenberg noted that he wanted to be in on the takeoffs as well as the crash landings. This is good advice even when the stakes are less momentous.

A case in point is the failure of President Clinton in early 1993 to gain congressional approval of his proposed $16.3 billion economic stimulus package, a center element of his overall economic plan. What blocked him was the unanimous opposition of the Senate Republicans, who had been all but ignored before the vote. Little effort had been made to sway or coopt them to win over at least a few centrists until it was too late. If the administration had worked with them from the outset, it might have been able to forge an overall majority.

Engaging your West makes it more likely that you will garner support; just as important, you may learn something that can be included in an initiative. California's 1992 reform of its health care system is a good example. At the time the reform effort began, 6 million Californians lacked health insurance, many of them employed by small businesses or related to someone working in one. The reform bill established a new statewide pool that made health care available to small businesses at a price they could afford; it was signed into law in July 1992 and took effect a year later. But long before the bill ever came up for a vote, Governor Pete Wilson held months of intense meetings—described by one participant as "group gropes"—between his administration and representatives of insurance companies, health maintenance organizations (HMOs), the business community, the state legislature, doctors, nurses, and hospitals. In the course of these discussions, the legislation changed—and support for it increased. And the process of interacting with the West did not end there. In July 1993, a year after signing the first bill, Wilson signed a second measure that assuaged the concerns of various associations that felt excluded by the initial legislation.

Develop and maintain relationships with influential people in your West. When I worked at the White House, I used to meet from time to time with my predecessors, in part to get ideas, but also to try to affect the thinking of those individuals who remained influential with both policy elites and the public. The same goes for powerful interest groups. Get to know them and their chief members. If need be, build a coalition of groups to help you counter or offset the opposition of others who cannot be brought on board. Without such efforts, you may find a united front against you. The failure of John Frohnmayer as chairman of the National Endowment of the Arts is telling in this regard. He alienated the conservatives who objected to some of the projects receiving funding, even as he angered the liberals, who felt he was not standing up for free expression. Without a base of support, he became ineffective and then vulnerable, and in the end he lost his job.[3]

So cultivate your West assiduously. But do not go too far. Listening to your West is important, but it is not the only thing; effectiveness requires equal parts leadership and management, and both involve equal parts directing and following. Depending on your philosophy, your agenda, and your relationships with your North, South, and East, you will have to determine whether to give way or to resist when your West pushes you. As Philip Selznick has written in his thoughtful book on the philosophy and practice of administration:

There is a difference between a university President who takes account of a state legislature or strong pressure groups and one who permits these forces to determine university policy. The leader's job is to *test* the environment to find out which demands can become truly effective threats, to *change* the environment by finding allies and other sources of external support, and to *gird* his organization by creating the means and the will to withstand attacks.[4]

Much of what makes up your West are groups or organizations built around a single (or at least narrow) set of aims. The media have their purposes, as do legislators, as does any lobby. Interest groups by definition are formed around interests. Special or single-issue groups are just that: they can pursue and promote one set of interests to the exclusion of all else. If you work in the public sector, you do not have that luxury. You will often have to say no; rarely will you be able to give an unconditional yes. At times, you will also have to end the debate and bring matters to a head for resolution. You should always hear people out, give them a chance to influence policy, incorporate what you agree to or can live with, and explain what you decided and why. Your West is a permanent part of your landscape and should be treated accordingly.

Relations with the Media

The media (including print and both television and radio) deserve special consideration as you look to your West. Their role is unique. They are both observers of and participants in the political process, but even when they are observing, they are participating. The media operate from an independent power base, and, although they cannot implement policies, they can affect perceptions on all four points of your compass and in the process help define what others see as desirable and feasible. Never underestimate the power of the media—and if you are in a position to influence them, you should work very hard to do so.

Many who work in government—or elsewhere in the public or private sector—tend to see the media as something of an enemy, if only because at times they will publish or broadcast stories that complicate their lives. This temptation to demonize or avoid the media is understandable. But either would be a mistake. In most cases, those in the media are just doing their job, a part of which is explaining why you are not doing yours well. As Christopher Matthews, once an aide to House Speaker Tip O'Neill, points out, "Always remember what these people do for a living. Their mission is to produce a good story, and in their business it's generally the bad news that makes the best headlines."[5]

Ignoring the media is self-defeating, for they will go ahead and air or publish stories all the same. For similar reasons, it rarely pays to fight them, because they are almost always going to have the last word. The media are a central, permanent, and powerful element of the political environment. Like any other constituency, they need to be managed. And if you do it right, you can move beyond damage limitation and promote your agenda. Paul Grogin, formerly of LISC, advocates a cooperative relationship with the media for precisely this reason:

We aggressively cultivated the real estate section of the *New York Times*, the Metro section, the other papers. There were any number of positive articles about this. A huge part of public entrepreneurship is working the press. It's another part of that echo effect that you want to generate. Obviously, you have to be careful about that. You can't be premature. You can't do it in a way that injures your boss or too blatantly exposes your agenda. But getting applause, editorially or in the way the news is covered at critical points along the way of a new undertaking, gives you an enormous advantage. Most people in the public sector don't do this very well. . . . It's really a very matter-of-fact thing. This is one of the things that needs demystifying. The press is people. If you understand what they're trying to do, what their needs are, you can provide services. I'm not talking about leaks. I'm talking about services for the press, in terms of their understanding issues. And in so doing, you become relied on as a good source of information and then at various opportunities you can get your agenda out there in a way that reinforces you.

Elizabeth Reveal, a former budget director in Washington, D.C., and a finance chief in Philadelphia, also worked hard to create a context in which an issue would get more accurate and understanding treatment from the media. It took considerable time, but it proved to be a worthwhile investment when financial issues came to dominate the local political scenes. She explains:

> I have always had really very good relations with the press, based on the same principles I have with elective legislators, and that is to try to be an educator at the same time that I am a source. And this is a good case in point. I was the budget director here [in Washington] four years after home rule. There isn't anybody in the Washington press corps who in those days understood anything about balanced budgets or real budget-making. They only knew the federal process. They only knew the expenditure side, did not know tax, did not know revenue, [so] I ran a very behind-the-scenes seminar twice a month for anybody who wanted to come. And we learned how to read balance sheets and we learned how to read the budget and we learned how to read a prospectus offering statement, and I did that for three years. And I got two or three people, sometimes five or six, depending on the issue. They never once violated the terms of those discussions. And they were open to anybody who wanted to come from the press and the people took advantage of it—got to be real good reporters of financial issues. And I did that in Philly, and it made a huge difference there.

You can increase public awareness of an issue by speaking to the media about it or by suggesting to some enterprising reporter that he or she might wish to look into a particularly interesting, unreported aspect of the issue. The media can also be useful for launching trial balloons. You can float the name of someone you're considering for an important position, and the reaction may help you decide whether to go ahead. Or you can float proposals and back away from one that gets too rough a reception. If you do this right, you can play a kind of media chess and create support for the initiative you really cared about all along. The Clinton administration did this in its initial budget reduction proposal, first floating dramatic changes in social security benefits, then "settling" for relatively modest changes in how benefits were taxed.

You can get your spin on a story—or see a policy undermined by the wrong spin. A classic example of negative spin is the debate over the neutron bomb, the weapons system proposed in the late 1970s that constituted a refinement of traditional battlefield nuclear weapons. The journalist who broke the story, Walter Pincus of the *Washington Post*, all but doomed the bomb's prospects by characterizing it as a weapon that killed people but left buildings intact. The neutron bomb was quickly caricatured as the ultimate capitalist weapon, one with more respect for goods than life. The Pentagon might have done much better if officials had briefed reporters about an innovation designed to reduce the destructive nature of war, one that would allow us, for instance, to kill enemy troops without destroying a city in the country of an ally that the Warsaw Pact had come to occupy.

Soon after taking office, the Clinton administration saw a negative perception beginning to develop and responded quickly. During the campaign, Clinton had spoken of the need for sacrifice if Americans wanted to reduce the budget deficit. But in the days before his initial budget address to the Congress, the word "sacrifice" began to disappear from the official lexicon, to be replaced by "contribution." Sacrifice sounds painful; contribution connotes civic-mindedness. All of this can get downright silly when taken to extremes—calling taxes "revenue enhancements" or the giant MX missile "the Peacekeeper"—but the language used to frame an issue dramatically affects the way it is perceived publicly.

In order to get the story told the way you want—or at least get it told in a way that will not cause major problems for you—it is crucial to choose your message and stick to it. This is not a suggestion to lie, which is never recommended, but sometimes it does mean answering not the question you were asked but the question you wish you had been asked. In some circumstances, getting your message out may mean refusing to answer a question no matter how often it is raised. You should also resist being drawn into answering hypothetical questions. These allow the journalist to set the agenda, and, if you are foolish enough to answer, you could create a problem where none exists or limit your options if the hypothetical situation ever materializes.

It is especially dangerous to ignore the media when you know that bad news is about to come out. The temptation is to duck, to avoid association with a failure or setback. But silence only increases the risk that the failure will look even worse than it is and perhaps be blamed on you to boot. Take as a model the way Attorney General Janet Reno made herself available for press and television interviews on the evening of the debacle in Waco, Texas; she got her perspective front and center and earned respect for having the courage to take responsibility for a policy failure. Contrast this with the way the Nixon administration failed to deal with what became Watergate or the way the Clinton White House allowed the story about problems in its travel office to drag on, with new and damaging revelations appearing every day. The lesson is obvious: if there is bad news, better get it out and over with quickly. Moreover, if you are very slow to get out bad news, you risk allowing a damaging story to be overtaken by a potentially worse one, that of incompetence, cover-up, or both.

Sometimes a crisis comes out of the blue, and no preparation is possible. But on other occasions—say, a major policy departure—there is no excuse for not addressing (and shaping) public perceptions. The failure of the Bush administration to prepare the way for its about face on taxes accounts for a good deal of its loss of public support. The question is not whether Bush was right to make "no new taxes" a major theme or whether he was right to alter his stance in June 1990. The point is simply that the change in policy would have met with a better reception if the president had gone on national television and explained why he believed new taxes were necessary. It is always better to get in front of a parade than to be trampled by it.

Cultivating the media can also help you shape expectations and set the standards by which your own performance will be judged. Done correctly, this can help you a great deal in the effort to build public support for your agenda. But the sword is double-edged: a general who promises to liberate a town by a certain date while incurring only so many casualties is setting himself up for a fall if he cannot deliver. Similarly, Peter Ueberroth did himself no favor when he named the organization created in the aftermath of the spring 1992 riots in Los Angeles "Rebuild LA." The group did some good, but it could never live up to the expectation that it would generate the resources needed to rebuild the city. That this expectation was unrealistic is beside the point; what matters here is that presentation can substantially affect perception and reaction.[6]

More generally, how you are treated in the media will also affect how you are perceived by your colleagues, bosses, and staff. Critical articles will almost certainly hurt you; but if you are a senior official, you probably should be getting some kind of coverage or you risk being dismissed by insiders and outsiders as someone who is "not a player." At the other extreme, too much attention and flattery will create suspicions that your cultivation of the press has gone too far—especially if you are not a senior official. Do what you can to keep the media's focus on your agenda and what you are doing to make it a reality, and you will have little to regret.

You can increase the odds of getting a desired story to appear by cooperating with a reporter. If it is television, pictures become central; you can help by proposing an interesting backdrop or by making one available. Deadlines matter, too. It does not help to get in touch with a television reporter who is just about to go on the air or with a print reporter so late in the day that it is too late to get a story into the next day's paper. Do your homework, learn the reporters' schedules, and do what you can to accommodate them.

I do not recommend using leaks to cultivate the media. "Leaking"—the unauthorized disclosure of information—is done for any number of purposes: to undermine an option or decision by premature or incomplete disclosure, to satisfy ego, to weaken an adversary. The results, however, tend to be the same. Leaking destroys trust and invariably leads to a narrowing of those involved in the decisionmaking process. In the long run, personal relationships and the quality of the policy both suffer. The best way to determine whether passing a particular piece of information to a reporter would constitute leaking is to think about how you would feel if your bosses and colleagues learned that you were the source. If this prospect makes you uncomfortable, you should probably keep the information to yourself.

By contrast, an authorized leak is better understood as a "plant." Mike McCurry, spokesman for President Bill Clinton for several years, used plants to great effect. "He would give one news organization a break on an upcoming development and it was certain to get big play, leaving the other reporters to play catch-up. Few journalists could resist the urge to breathlessly trumpet 'the President will announce tomorrow. . . . ' They looked like well-wired insiders, and the White House got a two-day bounce."[7]

Be sure you have an understanding with your boss about interacting with the media. If you are permitted to talk with reporters, it is vital that you do so with great care. Dealing with the media is similar to attending a meeting: you need to think through beforehand what you want to accomplish and how to get it done. You cannot control what is written or how a story is presented, but you can control whether you speak to the media, to whom, when, and most important, what you say. If you do your job right and if the journalist is a professional, you should not choke on your corn flakes when you pick up the morning paper.

Beware, too, of being clever or glib. L. William Seidman, the former head of the Federal Deposit Insurance Corporation (FDIC), recounts the tale of one proposal by the Bush administration to charge bank and S&L depositors a fee when they opened a new savings account. Asked by a reporter what he thought about the idea (which was designed to finance deposit insurance losses), Seidman remarked that the proposal "was a reversal from days past when a depositor could expect to be awarded a toaster for opening a new account. Now, instead of receiving a toaster, a new depositor would have to buy one for the bank." The White House was not amused; Seidman never quite recovered from a rash of stories about the "reverse toaster tax."[8]

Whatever you plan to say, always make sure the ground rules are understood by everyone involved. Traditionally, you can speak to the media under any of several conditions:

On the record. This is the Miranda equivalent; namely, everything you say can and will be used against you—and you means You, by name. These are the highest stakes. It is the preferred ground rule for the journalist, for it leaves no question as to the source. But just because a journalist wants you to go on the record, you do not have to agree. Indeed, most people working in the public sector do not have this option unless they are the designated spokesperson for their organization. If you do agree to go on the record and you are not the designated spokesperson, you should arrange to approve any quotes before they appear in a story.

On background. This allows the journalist to quote or paraphrase what you say and attribute it to an unnamed source, such as an administration official or spokesperson. Make sure you agree in advance what description will be used. Your purpose is to offer authoritative information without giving away its source. This approach has less impact than a statement given on the record— information from unnamed sources is easier for anyone to deny or contradict—but it gives you more latitude to get something out that needs airing. Beware, though, of speaking on background to any reporter you do not know or who has a reputation for not honoring ground rules, and remember as well that nothing is guaranteed to remain on background, especially if you make too much news. Peter Tarnoff, the Clinton State Department's number-three man, gave what he thought was a background briefing to journalists over lunch in mid-May 1993. He spoke to the press just as the Clinton administration was deciding not to get involved significantly in the former Yugoslavia, and what he said about the likely reduction in the U.S. role in the world was perceived as so newsworthy that it soon became common knowledge that Tarnoff was the source.

On deep background. In this case, you are permitting the journalist to use something you said but not to attribute it, even to an anonymous source. Often the information you provide is simply asserted or offered as the reporter's own thought or statement. This is another way to get an issue out in the public domain, but because no actual quotes are used and there is no link to an insider, information given on these terms tends to have even less impact.

Off the record. Under this ground rule, the reporter cannot use any of the information you provide in any form at all. Use this approach sparingly. Journalists do not like it because you are not really helping them write their story. Sometimes, however, a journalist is looking for guidance and is willing to let you speak off the record, if only so you can help him or her avoid making a horrible mistake. Still, be careful when talking off the record: once something is said, it can take on a life of its own, and a second journalist who hears of your comments may not feel constrained by ground rules he or she never agreed to.

Again, be sure to establish ground rules and agree on what they mean before talking with a journalist. These preliminaries may be awkward, especially if you and the journalist are friendly, but any awkwardness is better experienced before rather than after the fact. David Stockman, Ronald Reagan's first budget chief, probably should have come to a clearer understanding with William Greider before he spoke so disparagingly of the Reagan economic policy in an article that became a sensation when it appeared in the December 1981 issues of the *Atlantic*; had Stockman been more careful, he might have saved himself a trip to Ronald Reagan's woodshed. Similarly, it is difficult to believe that Leon Panetta, Bill Clinton's director of the Office of Management and the Budget, carefully considered the ground rules before he went on the record and, in a fit of misplaced candor early in his tenure, described several important Clinton initiatives as all but doomed.[9]

I have learned some of these lessons the hard way, and the following story is as personal as it was painful. In late 1990, several months into the Persian Gulf crisis, my wife invited another couple, old friends of hers who happened to be journalists, over for dinner. I was working at the White House at the time, and inevitably the conversation turned to the crisis in the Gulf. The discussion got intense, and I came on strong—too strong, it turns out—while describing the administration's thinking. Afterward, I asked my wife whether I needed to reinforce the ground rules I had casually set at dinner. She assured me that of course a conversation among friends over dinner was off the record and that we would insult them if we made this more explicit. A few days later, our dinner conversation became a front-page story in a major newspaper, and one of our guests was all over television with his scoop. One could do worse in this regard than heed the advice of Marlin Fitzwater, spokesman for President George Bush. "Reporters are always reporters. Only secondarily are they your friends. It's a twenty-four-hour-a-day occupation and you should never expect them to be anything else."[10]

Legislatures, Councils, and Congress

Congress (or any legislature) also deserves special consideration and treatment. As is often the case with the media or other independent and frequently difficult actors, one tends to avoid dealing with the legislative branch unless necessary. (Hale Champion, when asked whether he preferred being a dean in a private or public university, answered, "On the whole, I'd rather deal with the legal problems of dead men's money than with live legislators.") Legislators and their staffs can be demanding, intrusive, unfair, partisan, petty, and unreasonable. Yet none of these is a reason to ignore them, for they can have a great impact on your effectiveness with your West as well as with the other points of your compass. Legislators can also be creative and fair-minded and valuable allies, so ignoring them can be an opportunity lost. Brent Scowcroft's comments on Congress express the ambivalence felt by many in the executive branch:

> When I [first became] National Security Advisor, I looked at Congress as kind of a necessary evil. My job was fundamentally to advise the president, and it was up to [the office of] congressional relations to deal with Congress. In the interim, I decided that was a mistake, and that it was important to maintain a liaison, at least with certain members of Congress. By and large as a group they are very susceptible to flattery, if you will. And therefore I'd call them from time to time, certainly return their calls, try to be helpful. It would pay off, especially with the Sam Nunns and the Steve Solarzes—the kinds of people that I felt were susceptible to reasoned discourse and not simply solidly ideological, where it would be a waste of time.

There are formal and informal ways of influencing those elected to serve. The formal might consist of hearings and testimony; the informal might be a conversation on the phone or over a drink. Particularly when there is good news, allow them to share the credit. Legislators, more than most people, do not like to be surprised, especially when it involves an issue for which they have special responsibilities or that has significant consequences for their district. Senator Sam Nunn, someone relatively hawkish on defense matters, might have been expected to support the Bush administration's decision to use force to oust the Iraqis from Kuwait. Yet he did not, and his reported displeasure at being inadequately consulted on the decision to double the number of U.S. forces in the Gulf theater probably did not increase his disposition to go along with the administration.

Informal relations with Congress or any legislature are often more important and productive. Identify the most important members and staff and spend time with them, find out what matters to them. On every issue in every legislative body there are those to whom others turn for guidance on how to vote. Cultivate these experts: you will learn from them, and if you can persuade them of the wisdom of your views, you will have gone a long way toward persuading the majority of their colleagues. After all, what they say and how they vote can have a decisive impact on the fate of your agenda.

Informal ties can also be critical in building working relations with your West even when—or particularly when—you disagree. As former senator and 1992 Democratic presidential candidate Paul Tsongas said, "You never know where your next coalition is coming from." Former Massachusetts governor William Weld recounts how he and his political opposition agreed to reach out—and both gained as a result:

> The personal relationship with the [legislative] leadership is terribly important. In March of my first year, 1991, the Speaker [of the Massachusetts House of Representatives] and I both perceived that things were not getting off on the right track. We were publicly accusing each other of this, that and the other. So we had a secret breakfast. . . . Out of that arose a custom that we've adhered to religiously ever since then, of getting together every Monday, the leadership in the legislature of both parties, plus the Ways and Means chairmen, plus the Lieutenant Governor and myself. We get together every Monday at 3:15 p.m. for an hour and a half. We just talk about what's coming up that week, what's coming up that month, what somebody had for breakfast—whatever we want to talk about. And it makes it more difficult to stab a guy in the back or the chest if you know you are going to be sitting across the table from him, at the latest, seven days from today in a friendly, coffee-and-cookies setting, which is what those settings are.

Kathleen Sheekey, formerly legislative director for Common Cause and codirector of the Advocacy Institute, also emphasizes the importance of forging relationships that can weather disagreements:

There is a favorite phrase that Common Cause uses that is very good—"No permanent friends, no permanent enemies." It's the way I like to approach the Congress, that a member who may not be with you on a particular issue may surface on another. As an effective lobbyist, you always walk in the door no matter what the nature of the disagreement is or how deep it is, and you want to walk out knowing that you can come back in. So it's about building relationships and forging coalitions.

You should also keep in mind that what you say and do can affect a legislator's thinking and even swing him or her to your side on a critical issue. Again, Sheekey is instructive:

> One of the things you've got to do is create that groundswell that makes it irresistible for legislators. They have to see that they are going to get something out of it. They're going to get public support, they're going to get media attention, they're going to get some praise, and when it's an issue when they also know they are going to get some heat on the other side, and are going to have to work very hard, they have to be able to balance that with what the rewards are going to be and who it is who is going to support them. You have to create an environment where it's worth the legislator's while to work hard for that cause.

You are also more likely to gain favor and support for your agenda by working with members and their staffs before policies are set in cement or launched before the public. Michael Dukakis argues that this is one of the most important things he learned from his first term as governor—a term that was followed by defeat and subsequent reelection:

> Most legislators I've worked with respond very positively to a chief executive who says, I want you to be deeply and actively involved in this right from the beginning. They care just as much as you do. You don't have an exclusive lock on virtue. . . . One of the things I said to my people the second

time around is that we never start down a policy road without involving key legislators from the beginning. I never want to see anything in here on the policy side where we have not involved key committee chairs, key folks, from the beginning. First, because it will be better because they're involved because they know stuff that we don't know. And secondly, because if they're part of it, then they're going to be our spear carriers on the floor. Why did it take one term, a defeat and four years of thinking about it to wake up to that? Beats the hell out of me. . . . Defeat is a great teacher.

Passing laws is only one of the functions of legislative bodies, and not necessarily the most important. Legislators are there to hold hearings, to force the executive branch to be accountable, to demonstrate to the voters back home that they are living up to expectations. To some legislators, appearances matter most: introducing a bill, making a statement on the floor of the chamber, or offering a sound bite to the media that makes their local newscast can sometimes be more important than actually getting something accomplished. Legislators of every stripe are there, not simply to promote policies, but also to service their constituents, please special interests—and get reelected.

For government officials, public hearings require special caution. As former defense secretary Dick Cheney once said, "Those guys over there are not genuine listeners. They want to get on the record with their views and we should get on the record with ours. But don't look at testimony as a serious dialogue between questioners and witnesses."[11] Hearings are a forum and should be treated that way; the serious business of negotiating and politicking almost always takes place elsewhere.

Part of being realistic about hearings means understanding that some participants will want to score points at your expense. Don't allow yourself to be a punching bag; remember that you can posture for the press and public just as much as they can. James Baker is characteristically direct on the need to resist your West if warranted:

Make sure you stroke them to the extent that they need to be stroked, let them know how important they are and that you are conscious of their importance to the process, but you don't let them bully you. They may not say so publicly, but I think that they admire people who say what they think, that are willing to stand up. The worst thing in the world anybody can do in my opinion as a cabinet officer is go up to a hearing and take a bunch of crap from a congressman sitting up there posturing for the thirty-second spot on the evening news. He's co-equal, but he isn't any more equal, and you're not up there to take abuse. On a number of occasions I said I didn't come up here to listen to that kind of stuff, and normally they'll back down and apologize.

The challenge of working with the legislative branch will not yield to a simple solution. On some issues you will have an ally, on others, an adversary. It helps if you understand the legislator's political requirements. A member of Congress normally opposed to defense spending is likely to be a stalwart supporter of a weapons system produced in a home state, just as senators worrying over deficits and concerned about the environment may have to oppose energy taxes if they come from the large western states, where automobiles and trucks are the principal means of getting around. As in any negotiation, learn what you can about the other person's position and avoid asking for something he or she cannot realistically give you.

Just as important, try to learn what the other side really cares about. One former official involved in a negotiation between Congress and Transportation Secretary Elizabeth Dole recounts this story involving the capital's National and Dulles airports:

> We needed probably about 600 million to a billion dollars for construction and expansion. National needed massive rehabilitation and modernization. As long as they were part of the federal government, it was going to be tough to find the resources to do the kind of modernization that was necessary. Elizabeth Dole fought hard to transfer those airports to

an independent local authority. The airport wanted to go. The airlines wanted to go, because they knew that was the only way they were going to get expansion. The noise advocates, the neighborhood surrounding groups, did not want to see it. Baltimore-Washington Airport, BWI, didn't want to see it because they did want to see these two [other airports] grow. . . . How did you get Congress to go along? Elizabeth Dole sat in a room up off the Capitol with charts showing where the congressmen's parking places were going to be.

As general guidance for dealing with any legislators, you could do a lot worse than live by the rules set out by Patricia Clarey, previously a mid-level official in the National Park Service. In that post, she was called on to advise its new director, a state park director from Indiana who had never before worked with Congress. Clarey's guidelines were few but clear:

Be good to your members. Be truthful. If they are of another party, it doesn't matter, they might vote with you some time. If they don't vote with you the first time, it doesn't mean that they will not vote with you the second time. Don't burn those bridges early. Some members will never do anything for you, but it doesn't do you any good to alienate them further.

What all these comments about dealing with the legislative branch have in common is worth noting: honesty, attention, cultivating long-term relationships, inclusion, dependability. These traits and priorities will stand you in good stead as you build effective relations with other aspects of your West. Congress and state legislatures—or city councils and school boards—are no different, only more difficult.

Speaking out in Public

Communicating effectively with the public is crucial. Lobbyists and special interest groups will often seek you out. Individual citizens may also try to communicate directly. Even when they do not, you should make your way to them, for they can shape the political environment in which you work.

You can do this in several ways, ranging from the retail—phone calls, letters, small meetings—to the wholesale—large meetings, mailings, and speeches. If you choose to speak in public, all the realities of dealing with the press apply, except there is only one available ground rule: everything you say is on the record. Remember also that you are always representing not just yourself but your organization. Anything you say will be repeated—accurately if you are lucky, distortedly if you are not.

Writing letters can be a good way to make an impact on people you cannot meet. Many in the public sector tend to do the minimum, as captured cynically by a former congressional aide, Mark Bisnow:

> To my enduring benefit I quickly picked up the art of congressional letter writing. There seemed to be three essential attributes of the model reply. First, it should exhibit a personal touch—perhaps an opening salutation adapted to the recipient or an overall colloquial tone—that would leave the reader with the impression that the letter had been answered by the senator himself. Second, it should be restricted to descriptive or vaguely analytical discussion of an issue, thereby preventing the inconvenient documentation of a position on an issue that could later get the politician in trouble. And finally it should be extremely brief, permitting the letter writer to move on expeditiously to other correspondence.[12]

More creative (and time consuming) is the approach of James Strock, for years head of California's Environmental Protection Agency. Strock used incoming letters to learn about the interests and concerns of his constituents—"management by walking around" while still behind his desk—and, through his response, to persuade, educate, and signal that his agency was responsive:

I work hard to get back to people that have questions. It's so hard to deal with our bureaucracy. Call any part of California's government and ask some basic question—you'll get sent twenty places. So somebody calls here, they're going to get a response fast. At least they'll get a call back to say we can't do it yet but we're going to do it. We really try to be an advocate for common sense, for people's needs. I go through our correspondence carefully, probably beyond the normal. I learn a lot from it, particularly from people who aren't working for [organized special] interests. If they are personal letters that they have worked on, I write back myself by hand. I pay for these myself. I make clear they are not only getting the attention, but I am trying to show them we are not wasting money or anything else. Every little thing we can do that is nontraditional—that is more accountable, quicker, cheaper, simpler—I try to signal that in little ways. I stamp them myself. . . . It's an extra cost, it's a minor one, but it sends a signal I want to send.

Speeches are a particularly good tool for communicating, one that permits you to reach a large audience in a short space of time. Despite the risks they entail and the time they require, speeches offer an effective way of educating people about what you are doing and why. They can be used to create public support for a specific initiative or a general sense of good relations that may prove useful down the road. Speeches are especially important during crises, when people are hungry for information and guidance. Finally, speeches can help take the sting out of a policy if you are talking to an unhappy constituency. If the policy is tough, your words can compensate by being gentle, thereby letting your listeners know that you may disagree with them but do not dislike them.

Speeches have other potential benefits. Writing a speech can help you sort out your own thoughts on an issue you care about. Speeches also offer an opportunity to force the hand of your East; advocates of delaying a decision about a pending issue can be placed on the defensive. As Richard Reeves noted in his excellent biography of John Kennedy, "Speeches are policy; the drafting of speeches is the making of policy."[13]

Writing great speeches is an art; writing good speeches is a craft. The same can be said for delivery. The good news is that crafts can be taught and learned. You can learn how to incorporate alliteration and parallelism; with a little practice, you can become comfortable using metaphors and other rhetorical devices. You rarely err by being short. Peggy Noonan is adamant on this point in her memoir of her time writing speeches in the White House. "Remember the waterfront shack with the sign FRESH FISH SOLD HERE. Of course it's fresh, we're on the ocean. Of course it's for sale, we're not giving it away. Of course it's here, otherwise the sign would be someplace else. The final sign: FISH."[14]

Finding your own style as a speechmaker or speechwriter is not easy. My advice is not to force it, especially when starting out. Be yourself; anxiety causes many people to reach for the nearest cliché or to use unnatural techniques. As usual, Strunk and White are worth heeding: "Young writers often suppose that style is a garnish for the meat of prose, a sauce by which a dull dish is made palatable. Style has no such separate entity; it is nondetachable, unfilterable. The approach to style is by way of plainness, simplicity, orderliness, sincerity."[15] If you are writing speeches for someone else, take care that you do so in a manner that fits the person. I wrote numerous speeches and statements for George Bush and learned early that he would never use anything overly rhetorical or grandiose.

Technique is not everything. Never forget why you are giving the speech and to whom. William Safire tells an instructive story about writing a speech for Richard Nixon. As they worked on the final revisions, the president asked Safire what he thought the impact would be. Safire responded that there was "no news in it" and that "it's not going to set the world on fire." Nixon's response? "That's the whole object of our foreign policy, not to set the world on fire."[16]

A speech should always have a purpose, be it to launch an initiative, prepare the ground for one, build support for existing policy, or simply demonstrate that you are listening to the concerns of

the audience. It can be an important adjunct to what you are trying to accomplish. Give consideration as well to what your audience brings. You never want to talk down to an audience, but neither do you want to risk losing them by not taking the time to
provide a context and the necessary background. Former White
House aide Roger Porter explains why it is necessary to provide a
setting for your listeners:

> When people are inside government, they spend an enor-
> mous amount of time every day thinking about and worrying
> about issues, and thinking through all the ramifications of
> them. And there is a tendency that is almost unavoidable to
> assume that others are equally engaged in thinking about
> and worrying about these things. And that therefore when
> you say something, you can assume that your audience is
> hearing it in the same way that you are speaking it, and that
> they are picking it up, and that they are picking it up the first
> time. The reality is that people on the outside tune in and out
> episodically. They don't have the same background base, and
> they are picking up fragments, and from those fragments
> they are constructing an image.

Choose your words carefully, because a speech may have a shelf
life beyond the moment of its delivery. During the Gulf crisis, I
checked every statement I drafted for President Bush for how it
would be heard in Congress, in Baghdad, and in the capitals of our
coalition partners. Assume you do not have the luxury of telling
the audience what they want to hear without others' learning of
what you said; expect your words to reach other audiences that
might feel differently. Still, do not neglect the listeners in the hall.
Unlike those who may read the text later, your immediate audience
does not have the opportunity of rereading a line or stopping to
think. So provide structure, whether by numbering your points or
answering rhetorical questions you yourself pose, and repeat those
points you want people to remember. If real estate has three laws
(location, location, and location), then good public diplomacy has
its three: repetition, repetition, and repetition.

Conclusions

The specific composition of one's West inevitably varies, although for those in the public sector it tends to include governments of one kind or another, courts, interest groups, citizens, the media, and businesses. Whatever the combination, these entities possess considerable ability to influence your effectiveness, while your ability to influence them is mostly limited to persuasion. The key to success with your West is clear: early and regular engagement, honest communication, inclusion, taking the time to explain your views, making the effort to see things as others do, working to find compromises everyone can live with—and knowing when to draw a line. Many of the requirements for productive relations with your West are similar to those that work well with the other points of your compass.

Almost every investment you make to your West tends to be time and effort well spent. Your West is external only in the narrow sense: it may be outside your organization, but almost anyone to your West can enter your world and affect your relations with your boss, your staff, and your colleagues. Equally important, your West can make accomplishing your goals more or less difficult. Those to your West can become allies or adversaries. The West, more than any other point of the compass, creates the larger context in which you operate. Give it the attention it requires—and deserves.

7

Back to the Center

ON AUGUST 12, 1993, most newspapers and morning news shows highlighted the story of how the commandant of the Marines Corps, General Carl E. Mundy Jr., had been forced to rescind a directive instructing his recruiters to limit and, within two years, to reject married applicants. Mundy's directive, which also called for mandatory premarital counseling for any marine, was greeted with scorn and ridicule by numerous editorial writers and members of Congress. A chastened Mundy dutifully apologized for having "blindsided" his bosses (who were reported to have been astonished over the order). Speaking to the media, he said: "I did not adequately inform my civilian superiors of the policy that I was putting forth. It's as simple as that."[1]

But was it? Certainly Mundy ought to have shown a draft of the directive to his superiors, but it would only have resulted in his being rebuked quietly rather than publicly. He would have saved himself some embarrassment but accomplished nothing in the way of either increasing reenlistment rates or decreasing divorce rates for married marines—the two concerns that led him to issue the directive in the first place.

What might the general have done? First, he ought to have determined whether limiting marriages of young marines was a priority worth fighting for. If that was indeed his conclusion, he and his staff should have examined the problem more rigorously to make sure it was as damaging as Mundy seemed to believe and that his proposed solution was demonstrably better than any realistic alternative. He should have held preliminary consultations not only with his bosses but also with Congress. Assuming the responses were encouraging, he could have tested the issue in the media and with the public, which would have increased their receptivity to new approaches while alerting him to those options that had the least appeal. If the general had approached his colleagues in the other armed services, he might have enlisted some important allies. Conversations with rank-and-file marines might have produced other ideas, new support for his preferred solution, or both. Hearings, or the establishment of a commission, might have provided a useful forum to study the idea further, scrub some of the possible options, and, finally, build consensus for the adoption and implementation of a workable policy.

In short, General Mundy might have had more success if he had used a mental compass as a tool to help him build alliances and persuade a majority of the powers-that-be to effect the change he desired. Good intentions, creative ideas, above-average intelligence, hard work—all of these are not enough to guarantee success in the world of politics, a world characterized by a broad distribution of power and authority. Navigating this terrain successfully—accomplishing ends that produce public good— is difficult. But using a compass designed to suit your working environment will help. Mapping the points of your compass— identifying all those to your North, South, East, and West—can make it easier to devise a strategy for determining what needs to be done and then translating objectives into accomplishments.

Effective performance requires constant interaction between you, the center of your compass, and its four points. Remember: Your success with each of your four compass points will affect your ability to persuade the other three. Thus your ability to influence your North will in part be a consequence of how well you can draw on your South and shape your East and West; equally, your ability to make the most of your South and influence colleagues and groups to your East and West will in part reflect how much influence you wield with your North. You do not have the luxury to focus on only one direction of your compass; your success with one can beget success with others, just as failure with one can hurt you not just directly but everywhere.

Interaction with all four compass points is important for a second reason. Philosophy alone cannot dictate your agenda. Exposing your tentative agenda to your compass points is a critical step in refining what you seek to accomplish. By testing your ideas with others—bosses, staff, colleagues, outsiders—you increase the odds that you will be effective. A proposal that has not been exposed to the bureaucratic or political marketplace is more likely to be flawed than one that has withstood scrutiny and possibly been modified as a result. This constant interaction between you and your political environment is critical. Purpose must shape power and vice versa.

Interaction with all the points of your compass has still another benefit. Close relationships, not simply with bosses and subordinates, but also with colleagues and interest groups, are central to building support for the adoption and implementation of your proposals. People are much more willing to support some innovation or enterprise if they have had a chance to shape it and if they understand its origins and its purposes. Expanding participation and practicing inclusion are the best way to promote implementation—without which the policy might just as well not exist in the first place.

Working your compass thus provides both a means of determining what needs to be done and a means of getting it done. In fact, the process that leads to better policy development is the same process that leads to better policy implementation. Both require steady interaction between you, the center of the compass, and your political environment, your North, South, East, and West.

If you follow these principles, you are likely to discover that effectiveness is available to anyone, anywhere. Any position brings with it the opportunity to be heard, to speak, to manage, to lead. All too often we tend to think of managing or leading as coming from the top down, something that those high on the ladder do for and to those lower down. This is not wrong, but it is incomplete. *The management and leadership of those who work for you is a major responsibility, but you can also manage and lead your bosses, your colleagues, and your external environment.* You can lead—you must lead—from below in shaping the behavior of those to your North and from the side in shaping the thinking and behavior of colleagues and interest groups and other organizations to your East and West.

But wanting to exert influence and exerting influence are two very different things. What does it take? Throughout the course of this book, five essential principles turn up at regular intervals. Like many basic ideas, they may seem obvious; but like many obvious things, they are all too easy to overlook amid the intensity of the crisis—or the boredom of the day-to-day.

The Five Principles

1. Develop and focus on a narrow agenda.

Working alone and with others, concentrate your efforts on those few things that you have determined are desirable and achievable given your circumstances—that is, given your philosophy, the resources at your command, and the constraints. Having a keen sense of what you want to accomplish most and where you want to go is a prerequisite for all else.

2. Look for opportunities to act.

Do not run away from doing things. Assert authority, take risks, and fight if need be for what is central to your agenda.

3. Bring honesty and integrity to all that you do.

This applies to both the intellectual and the personal realms. You need to speak truth to power, to give your boss and your colleagues your best advice. And you need to conduct your relations with people around you—above, below, to the side—so that what you say and do may be challenged on substance but not on truthfulness. Being effective is hard enough without becoming your own hurdle.

4. Be aware.

Be careful with facts, mindful of assumptions, rigorous in your analysis, mindful of the consequences of what you are about to do or say or write. Prepare thoroughly; follow through just as thoroughly. A great deal can be undone by carelessness or sloppiness of any sort.

5. Pay attention to people.

Personal relationships are often the key to effectiveness. Living by this rule runs the gamut from studying those you work for and deciding whom to hire to negotiating with your colleagues and meeting with interest groups. Being smart is rarely enough; ideas, no matter how good, rarely if ever sell themselves. Wherever possible, work with these people, include them, listen to them, both to improve the quality of the work at hand and to increase the chance that the policies you seek will be approved and implemented faithfully.

Being effective is that simple—and that complicated. So check your compass from time to time. Begin at the center with yourself, then review all four directions—North, South, East, and West. Examine your relationships with your boss, your staff, your colleagues, and all others around you. Then return to the center. Ask yourself whether you are still on course. Repeat this evaluation every few months, more frequently when you encounter resistance or feel frustration. There is no better way to demonstrate that bureaucracy and entrepreneurship can go hand in hand.

Suggestions
for Further
Reading

THERE EXISTS A VAST and growing literature on business management, public administration, and public policy, not to
mention all the memoirs, biographies and histories of people and
events. What follows is a select, annotated list of books that I recommend to those who want to read on.

Acheson, Dean, *Present at the Creation: My Years in the State Department*
(W. W. Norton, 1969). These memoirs by Truman's secretary of state
are a cut above most of the genre. His conclusion (chapter 76,
"Summing Up") makes a good many good points about the business of
making policy.

Altshuler, Alan A., and Robert D. Behn, eds. *Innovation in American Government: Challenges, Opportunities, and Dilemmas* (Brookings, 1997).
Chapter 16, by Ellen Schall, is a gem that contains as much wisdom
per page as any other work on management in the public sector.

Augustine, Norman R. *Augustine's Laws* (New York: American Institute of
Aeronautics and Astronautics, 1982). Do not let the procurement case
studies put you off; Augustine, formerly CEO of Lockheed Martin, has
keen insights and a dry sense of humor.

Birnbaum, Jeffrey H., and Alan S. Murray. *Showdown at Gucci Gulch:
Lawmakers, Lobbyists, and the Unlikely Triumph of Tax Reform* (Random
House, 1987). One of the best case studies of Washington in action,

involving Congress, the executive, and lobbyists as they worked over the Reagan tax reform proposals.

Bisnow, Mark. *In the Shadow of the Dome: Chronicles of a Capitol Hill Aide* (New York: William Morrow, 1990). An insider account by a former congressional aide as he goes from job to job.

Bronner, Ethan. *Battle for Justice: How the Bork Nomination Shook America* (W. W. Norton, 1989). The best case study of this historic political battle.

Buckley, James. *If Men Were Angels: A View from the Senate* (Putnam, 1975). A fascinating and fun look at a typical week in the life of a U.S. senator.

Burns, James MacGregor. *Leadership* (Harper & Row, 1978). One of the principal works in the field.

Califano, Joseph A. Jr. *The Triumph & Tragedy of Lyndon Johnson: The White House Years* (Simon & Schuster, 1991). My favorite account of the Johnson era, one rich in anecdotes.

Caro, Robert A. *Robert Moses and the Fall of New York* (Knopf, 1974). One of the great biographies of a larger-than-life figure who got things done, if not always the right things and if not always in ways that look admirable by today's standards.

Chase, Gordon, and Elizabeth C. Reveal. *How to Manage in the Public Sector* (Random House, 1983). This highly readable book provides wise and practical advice to insiders.

— Cohen, William A. *The Art of the Leader* (Englewood Cliffs, N.J.: Prentice Hall, 1990) One of the better examples of the many works devoted to this subject.

Covey, Stephen R. *The 7 Habits of Highly Effective People* (Simon & Schuster/Fireside, 1989). I brought more than a little skepticism to this book. I am glad to admit I was wrong.

Cuomo, Mario. *Forest Hills Diary: The Crisis of Low Income Housing* (Random House, 1974) A young Mario Cuomo, then a lawyer pulled into a fierce local political struggle, shares the details of consensus building as well as his own doubts and reactions. This is a very good small book.

Drucker, Peter F. *Managing the Non-Profit Organization: Principles and Practices* (HarperCollins, 1990) The only one of the master's works devoted entirely to the nonbusiness world.

Edwards, George C. *Implementing Public Policy* (Washington, D.C.: Congressional Quarterly Press, 1980). A straightforward treatment of the requirements of implementation.

Ehrenhalt, Alan. *The United States of Ambition: Politicians, Power, and the Pursuit of Office* (Random House, 1991). This is an important book, one that shows how we are led by self-selected career politicians.

Fenno, Richard F., Jr. *Learning to Govern: An Institutional View of the 104th Congress* (Brookings, 1997). As the title suggests, this is a primer on governing (as opposed to campaigning).

Fernandez, Joseph A., with John Underwood. *Tales Out of School: Joseph Fernandez's Crusade to Rescue American Education* (Boston: Little, Brown, 1993). A revealing account by the former head of both Miami's and New York City's public schools.

Frankel, Charles. *High on Foggy Bottom: An Outsider's Inside View of the Government* (Harper & Row, 1968). A delightful and charming memoir that looks at the State Department much as a good anthropologist might study some strange tribe.

Gardiner, John. *On Leadership* (Free Press, 1990). A good book by a practitioner who has reflected on public service.

Goddard, Taegan D., and Christopher Riback. *You Won Now What? How Americans Can Make Democracy Work from City Hall to the White House* (Simon & Schuster, 1999). A useful and readable discussion of the challenges of governing.

Goldhamer, Herbert. *The Advisor* (New York: Elsevier, 1978) A thorough look at the role of advisors throughout history.

Gordon, George J. *Public Administration in America* (St. Martin's Press, 1986). One of the better academic texts.

Hamilton, Alexander, James Madison, and John Jay. *The Federalist Papers* (New York: New American Library, 1961). Essential reading to understand American history and politics.

Heller, Joseph. *Good as Gold* (London: Jonathan Cape, 1979). Heller's Bruce Gold is a classic character whose encounter with a Nixon-like White House is cynical, funny, and insightful.

Heymann, Philip B. *The Politics of Public Management* (Yale University Press, 1987). This book, written by a Harvard Law professor who went on to serve as the number-two person at the Clinton Department of Justice, uses many of the cases central to the public policy management curriculum at Harvard's Kennedy School.

Hoving, Thomas. *Making the Mummies Dance: Inside the Metropolitan Museum of Art* (Simon & Schuster, 1993). I cannot judge the accuracy of Hoving's account, but it is a fascinating glimpse into the politics of one public institution.

Johnson, Haynes, and David S. Broder. *The System: The American Way of Politics at the Breaking Point* (Boston: Little, Brown, 1996). By far the best postmortem on the Clinton health care reform failure.

Kelman, Steven. *Making Public Policy: A Hopeful View of American Politics* (Basic Books, 1987). Kelman, with whom I taught at Harvard and who went on to oversee procurement policy at the Clinton Office of Management and Budget, has written a thoughtful and upbeat book. His treatment of governing institutions is especially valuable.

Kingdon, John W. *Agendas, Alternatives, and Public Policies* (Boston: Little, Brown, 1984). One of the texts I used when teaching, Kingdon's book, while academic in style, is useful in describing how issues become ripe for political action.

Kotter, John P. *Power and Influence* (Free Press, 1985). A solid book that addresses relationships with bosses, staff, and colleagues.

Lax, David A., and James K. Sebenius. *The Manager as Negotiator: Bargaining for Cooperation and Competitive Gain* (Free Press, 1986). A serious academic study that integrates negotiations and public policy.

Lynn, Jonathan, and Antony Jay. *The Complete Yes Prime Minister* (London: BBC Books, 1986–87). Like its companion books and like the BBC television series, this book is not only hilarious but educational about politicians and politics.

Lynn, Laurence E., Jr. *Managing the Public's Business: The Job of the Government Executive* (Basic Books, 1981). This book is one of the best works on this subject.

Machiavelli, Niccolo. *The Prince* (Chicago: Henry Regnery, 1963 edition translated by A. Robert Caponigri). Often misunderstood, Machiavelli has much to say to modern readers about effective leadership, not manipulation.

Mansbridge, Jane J. *Why We Lost the ERA* (University of Chicago Press, 1986). A very good case study of how a movement was done in by poor strategy and tactics alike.

Matthews, Christopher. *Hardball: How Politics Is Played—Told by Someone Who Knows the Game* (New York: Summit Books, 1988). Lots of stories and handy maxims from Tip O'Neill's former aide.

McCullough, David. *Truman* (Simon & Schuster, 1992). Truman's letters provide a great deal of rich material about politics and policymaking in this first-rate biography.

Moynihan, Daniel P. *The Politics of a Guaranteed Income: The Nixon Administration and the Family Assistance Plan* (Random House, 1973). A well-written case study of politics within the executive branch, as well as with Congress and interest groups, by the former professor/bureaucrat/ ambassador turned senator.

Neustadt, Richard E. *Presidential Power and the Modern Presidents: The Politics of Leadership from Roosevelt to Reagan* (Free Press, 1990). The updated and, I am reliably told, final version of this contemporary classic brings as much insight to American politics as any other book.

Neustadt, Richard E., and Ernest R. May. *Thinking in Time: The Uses of History for Decision Makers* (Free Press, 1986). Contains helpful dos and don'ts for those who would use or abuse history in the course of analysis or advocacy.

Nicolson, Sir Harold. *Diplomacy* (London: Oxford University Press, 1969). An elegantly written essay that is not only enjoyable but also has much to say on modern negotiations.

Noonan, Peggy. *What I Saw at the Revolution* (Random House, 1990). A warm, funny, delightful book, all the more valuable because it is written from the modest perspective of a worker-bee, at the time a speechwriter in the Reagan White House.

Osborne, David. *Laboratories of Democracy* (Harvard Business School Press, 1988). An important book, one that focuses attention on what a number of states were doing to improve the quality of government and the services it provides.

Osborne, David, and Ted Gaebler. *Reinventing Government: How the Entrepreneurial Spirit Is Transforming the Public Sector* (Reading, Mass.: Addison-Wesley, 1992). Not as good as Osborne's earlier effort, this is nonetheless an influential treatise (especially with the Clinton administration) that argues for governments' adopting a new public/private paradigm.

Peters, Thomas J., and Robert H. Waterman Jr. *In Search of Excellence: Lessons from America's Best-Run Companies* (Harper & Row, 1982). Despite the fall of some of the successes, this book is still valuable, and many of its insights apply equally to the corporate and nonbusiness worlds.

Phillips, Donald T. *Lincoln on Leadership: Executive Strategies for Tough Times* (New York: Warner Books, 1992). A lot of good sense; Lincoln had a surprising amount to say on management.

Pressman, Jeffrey L., and Aaron Wildavsky. *Implementation* (University of California Press, 1973). The subtitle says it all: "How Great Expectations in Washington are Dashed in Oakland; or, Why It's Amazing that Federal Programs Work at all, this being a saga of the Economic Development Administration as told by two sympathetic observers who seek to build morals on a foundation of ruined hopes." An influential work on the subject.

Redman, Eric. *The Dance of Legislation* (Simon & Schuster, 1973). A good "how a bill became a law" tale told by a young congressional aide.

Reich, Robert B., ed. *The Power of Public Ideas* (Cambridge, Mass.: Ballinger, 1988). A collection of quality essays on public policy by many of my former colleagues, several of whom went on to become senior members of the Clinton administration.

Reich, Robert B. *Locked in the Cabinet* (Alfred A. Knopf, 1997). An entertaining and insightful memoir despite its excesses.

Reid, T. R. *Congressional Odyssey: The Saga of a Senate Bill* (New York: W. H. Freeman, 1980). Another well-written account, by a young *Washington Post* writer, of how a bill became law.

Safire, William. *Before the Fall: An Inside View of the Pre-Watergate White House* (Garden City, N.Y.: Doubleday, 1975). Not only well written (as you would expect), but filled with anecdotes and sprinkled with helpful hints about working in government.

Selznick, Philip. *Leadership in Administration: A Sociological Interpretation* (Evanston, Ill.: Row Peterson, 1957). A thoughtful and well-written analysis of the subject.

Sowell, Thomas. *A Conflict of Visions: Ideological Origins of Political Struggles* (New York: William Morrow, 1987). A provocative essay on the fundamentals that often drive day-to-day political debates and divisions.

Stockman, David A. *The Triumph of Politics: Why the Reagan Revolution Failed* (Harper & Row, 1986). A revealing (at times unintentionally, I suspect) insider account.

Strunk, William, Jr., and E. B. White. *The Elements of Style* (Macmillan, 1979). Still, and probably forever, the best investment for anyone wanting to learn how to write with clarity, economy and grace.

de Tocqueville, Alexis, *Democracy in America* (Random House, 1945). Essential reading for understanding American political culture.

Trattner, John H. *A Survivors' Guide for Government Executives: How to Succeed in Washington* (Lanham, Md: University Press of America, 1989). This thin book provides some practical advice to those entering federal government at middle levels.

Waldman, Steven. *The Bill: How Legislation Really Becomes Law: A Case Study of the National Service Bill* (New York: Penguin Books, 1995). One of the better of the genre describing "how a bill—or, more precisely, an idea—becomes a law."

Wilson, James Q. *Bureaucracy: What Government Agencies Do and Why They Do It* (Basic Books, 1989). Probably the most important contemporary book on the subject.

Wolf, Thomas. *Managing a Nonprofit Organization* (New York: Prentice Hall, 1990) Helpful nuts and bolts.

Woodward, Bob, and Scott Armstrong. *The Brethren* (New York: Avon, 1981). A look at the Supreme Court as a political rather than a sacred legal institution.

Wouk, Herman. *Inside, Outside* (Boston: Little, Brown, 1985). Like Heller's effort cited above, Wouk's novel often has more to teach about governing than many texts.

Zartman, I. William, and Maureen R. Berman. *The Practical Negotiator* (Yale University Press, 1982). Just as you might expect, a comprehensive "how to" for negotiators.

Notes

Preface

1. Peter F. Drucker, *The Effective Executive* (Harper Colophon, 1985).

2. All statistics are derived from U.S. Department of Commerce, *Statistical Abstract of the United States: 1998* (Government Printing Office, 1998).

3. John J. DiIulio Jr., Gerald Garvey, and Donald F. Kettl, *Improving Government Performance: An Owner's Manual* (Brookings, 1993), p. 79.

4. See the report issued by the Clinton administration's National Performance Review, *From Red Tape to Results: Creating a Government That Works Better & Costs Less* (Government Printing Office, 1993). Similar ideas can be found in both David Osborne and Ted Gaebler, *Reinventing Government: How the Entrepreneurial Spirit Is Transforming the Public Sector* (Reading, Mass.: Addison-Wesley, 1992); and John J. DiIulio Jr., Gerald Garvey, and Donald F. Kettl, *Improving Government Performance: An Owner's Manual* (Brookings, 1993). An earlier call for improving how government is run is Frederic V. Malek, *Washington's Hidden Tragedy: The Failure to Make Government Work* (Free Press, 1978). A more academic entry in this field is Michael Barzelay (with the collaboration of Babak J. Armajani), *Breaking Through Bureaucracy: A New Vision for Managing in Government* (University of California Press, 1992). Additional recent examples of reports urging public sector reform include the National Commission on the Public Service [the Volcker commission], "Leadership for America: Rebuilding the Public Service" (Washington,

D.C.: 1989); National Academy of Public Administration, "Leading People in Change: Empowerment, Commitment, Accountability" (Washington, D.C.: April 1993); and the National Commission on the State and Local Public Service, "Hard Truths/Tough Choices" (1993). Excerpts of the report of the National Commission (informally known as the Winter commission, after its chairman, former Mississippi governor William Winter) can be found in *Governing* (August 1993), pp. 48–56. A brief historical survey of such undertakings can be found in Ronald C. Moe, *Reorganizing the Executive Branch in the Twentieth Century: Landmark Commissions* (Washington, D.C.: Congressional Research Service, 1992).

Chapter 1

1. For one tale of woe showing how government service can turn your life upside down, see Elliott Abrams, *Undue Process: A Story of How Political Differences Are Turned into Crimes* (Free Press, 1993).

2. To get an idea of the politics of running a university, see Henry Rasovsky, "Deaning," *Harvard Magazine* (January-February 1987), pp. 34–40; Richard Berendzen, *Is My Armor Straight? A Year in the Life of a University President* (Bethesda, Md.: Adler & Adler, 1986); and A. Bartlett Giamatti, *A Free and Ordered Space: The Real World of Universality* (W. W. Norton, 1988). Rasovsky was a dean at Harvard; Berendzen was president of American University; Giamatti headed Yale. For a depiction of what it takes to run an elementary school, see Walt Harrington, "The Education of Cynthia Summers," *Washington Post Magazine*, October 24, 1993.

3. Quoted in Marjorie Williams, "Burden of Proof," *Washington Post Magazine*, April 11, 1993, p. 18.

4. Charles Frankel, *High on Foggy Bottom: An Outsider's Inside View of the Government* (Harper & Row, 1968), pp. 139–40.

5. Quoted in Richard E. Neustadt, *Presidential Power and the Modern Presidents: The Politics of Leadership from Roosevelt to Reagan* (Free Press, 1990), p. 37.

6. James Chace, *Acheson: The Secretary of State Who Created the American World* (Simon & Schuster, 1998), p. 387.

7. Thomas Hoving, *Making the Mummies Dance: Inside the Metropolitan Museum of Art* (Simon & Schuster, 1993), p. 15.

8. Sir Harold Nicolson, *Diplomacy* (London: Oxford University Press, 1969), p. 67.

9. Vaclav Havel, "Paradise Lost," *New York Review of Books*, April 9, 1992, p. 7.

10. William Safire, *Before the Fall: An Inside View of the Pre-Watergate White House* (Garden City, N.Y.: Doubleday, 1975), p. 14.

11. The applicability of TQM to the public sector is a question that has produced more than a little controversy. A range of largely sympathetic views is included in "Forum on Improving Government Performance" in the *Public Manager*, vol. 21, no. 4 (Winter 1992–93), pp. 4–27. Also largely sympathetic (despite the title) is a short piece by David Osborne, "Why Total Quality Management Is Only Half a Loaf," *Governing* (August 1992), p. 65. The essence of TQM can be found in W. Edwards Deming, *Out of the Crisis* (MIT Center for Advanced Engineering Study, 1986). For relatively critical assessments of TQM, see Jonathan Walters, "The Cult of Total Quality," *Governing* (May 1992), pp. 38–42; and James E. Swiss, "Adapting Total Quality Management (TQM) to Government," *Public Administration Review* (July/August 1992), pp. 356–62.

12. Peter F. Drucker, *Managing the Non-profit Organization: Principles and Practices* (Harper Collins, 1990), p. 107.

13. Frankel, *High on Foggy Bottom*, p. 81.

14. Peter F. Drucker, *The Age of Discontinuity: Guidelines to Our Changing Society* (Harper & Row, 1968), p. 236.

15. James Q. Wilson, *Bureaucracy: What Government Agencies Do and Why They Do It* (Basic Books, 1989), pp. 317–18.

16. Ibid.

17. The quotation is from an interview of W. Michael Blumenthal, "Candid Reflections of a Businessman in Washington." It was conducted by Herman Nickel and appeared in *Fortune*, vol. 99, no. 2 (January 29, 1979), pp. 45–46.

18. George P. Shultz, *Turmoil and Triumph: My Years as Secretary of State* (Scribner's, 1993), pp. 34–35.

19. Neustadt, *Presidential Power*, p. 29.

20. David McCullough, *Truman* (Simon & Schuster, 1992), pp. 484–85.

21. Ibid., p. 914.

22. Here I made liberal use of a thoughtful and wonderfully titled unpublished paper by Graham T. Allison, "Administrative Leadership, Public and Private: Are They Fundamentally Alike in All Unimportant Respects?" (Cambridge, Mass.: July 1981). Laurence E. Lynn Jr. also discusses this question at length in his *Managing the Public's Business: The Job of the Government Executive* (Basic Books, 1981), ch. 5.

Chapter 2

1. Jeffrey H. Birnbaum, *Madhouse: The Private Turmoil of Working for the President* (Random House, 1996), pp. 38–39.

2. Robert B. Reich, *Locked in the Cabinet* (Alfred A. Knopf, 1997), pp. 335–36.

3. For a friendly critique of the state of education and training in this field, with a focus on Harvard's Kennedy School, see Derek Bok, "A Daring and Complicated Strategy," *Harvard Magazine*, May-June 1989, pp. 47–58.

4. Kristol has written an interesting article along these lines. See his "Can-Do Government: Three Reagan Appointees Who Made a Difference," *Policy Review* (Winter 1985), pp. 62–66.

5. John W. Kingdon, *Agendas, Alternatives, and Public Policies* (Boston: Little, Brown, 1984), p. 175.

6. Ibid., p. 115.

7. Mark H. Moore, *Accounting For Change: Reconciling the Demands for Accountability and Innovation in the Public Sector* (Washington, D.C.: Council for Excellence in Government, 1993), p. 155.

8. Alan A. Altshuler and Robert D. Behn, eds., *Innovation in American Government: Challenges, Opportunities, and Dilemmas*, (Brookings, 1997), p. 366.

9. See Jill Zuckman, "Senate Clears National Service Despite GOP Objections," *Congressional Quarterly*, September 11, 1993, p. 2397.

10. Isaiah Berlin, "The Hedgehog and the Fox," in *Russian Thinkers* (London: Pelican Books Edition, 1979), pp. 22–81. The title comes from the poetry of the Greek poet Archilochus: "The fox knows many things, but the hedgehog knows one big thing."

11. Mark H. McCormack, *What They Still Don't Teach You at Harvard Business School* (Bantam Books, 1989), p. 3.

12. Reeves quoted by Gerald Eskenazi, "Reeves Means Business, So Bring the Hard Hats," *New York Times*, August 26, 1993, p. B16.

13. William G. Pagonis with Jeffrey L. Cruikshank, *Moving Mountains: Lessons in Leadership and Logistics from the Gulf War* (Boston: Harvard Business School Press, 1992), p. 81.

14. See Stephen Labaton, "Firearms Agency Struggles to Rise from the Ashes of the Waco Disaster," *New York Times*, November 5, 1993, p. A7.

15. This excerpt is from the translation of Clausewitz's *On War* by Michael Howard and Peter Paret (Princeton University Press, 1976), p. 119.

16. See Haynes Johnson and David S. Broder, *The System: The American Way of Politics at the Breaking Point* (Boston: Little, Brown, 1996), pp. 4–9.

17. "Our Do-nothing Government," *New York Times*, March 30, 1992, p. A17.

18. Dean Acheson, *Present at the Creation: My Years in the State Department* (W. W. Norton, 1969), p. 731.

19. Steven Kelman, *Making Public Policy: A Hopeful View of American Government* (Basic Books, 1987), p. 292.

20. Quoted in David S. Broder and Dan Balz, "Clinton Finds Change Harder than Expected," *Washington Post*, May 14, 1993, p. A1.

21. David A. Stockman, *The Triumph of Politics: Why the Reagan Revolution Failed* (Harper & Row, 1986), pp. 101–02.

22. On this point see Kenneth J. Cooper, "Hill Turf Fights May 'Reinvent' Gore Proposals," *Washington Post*, September 13, 1993, p. A19; Gwen Ifill, "Gore's Views on Better Government May Be Easier to Utter Than Deliver," *New York Times*, September 5, 1993, p. 38; and Paul Glastris, "Whose Government is Gored?" *New Republic*, October 11, 1993, pp. 33–36.

23. Stephen R. Covey, *The 7 Habits of Highly Effective People* (Simon & Schuster, 1989), p. 161.

24. Ellen Schall, "Notes from a Reflective Practitioner of Innovation," in Altshuler and Behn, eds., *Innovation in American Government* (Brookings, 1997), p. 370.

25. Mario Cuomo, *Forest Hills Diary: The Crisis of Low Income Housing* (Random House, 1974), pp. 145–46.

26. Quoted in Frederick C. Klein, "On the Sidelines," *Wall Street Journal*, December 4, 1998, p. W9.

27. The alleged keys to Darman's success—"work harder than anybody else, be more prepared and add a dash of psychological intimidation; flatter up; get control of the paper; even if you believe in the power of the few, or the one, keep some proletarian touches; and dare to be petty," are described colorfully by Maureen Dowd, "A Primer: How the White House Budget Czar Not Only Survives, but Thrives," *New York Times*, September 22, 1992, p. A25.

28. Carl Bernstein and Marco Politi, *His Holiness: John Paul II and the Hidden History of Our Time* (Doubleday, 1996), p. 507.

Chapter 3

1. See Deborah Shapley, *Promise and Power: The Life and Times of Robert McNamara* (Boston: Little, Brown, 1993), pp. 85–86; and Edwin O. Guthman and Jeffrey Shulman, eds., *Robert Kennedy in His Own Words: The Unpublished Reflections of the Kennedy Years* (Bantam Books, 1988), pp. 34–36. The oral history project includes an account by Robert Kennedy of how his brother honored his agreement with McNamara and did not insist he hire Franklin Roosevelt Jr. as secretary of the Navy when McNamara objected.

2. Recounted in Hedrick Smith, *The Power Game: How Washington Works* (Random House, 1988), pp. 308–09. For Haig's version of this

episode, see his memoir, *Caveat: Realism, Reagan, and Foreign Policy* (Macmillan, 1984), pp. 74–76.

3. Dick Morris, *Behind the Oval Office: Winning the Presidency in the Nineties* (Random House, 1997), p. 241.

4. George P. Shultz, *Turmoil and Triumph: My Years as Secretary of State* (Scribner's, 1993), p. 27.

5. David A. Stockman, *The Triumph of Politics: Why the Reagan Revolution Failed* (Harper & Row, 1986), pp. 277–91.

6. Quoted in David McCullough, *Truman* (Simon & Schuster, 1992), p. 752.

7. Joseph Heller, *Good as Gold* (London: Jonathan Cape, 1979), pp. 52–53.

8. Quoted in Haynes Johnson and David S. Broder, *The System: The American Way of Politics at the Breaking Point* (Boston: Little, Brown, 1996), p. 286.

9. Admiral William J. Crowe Jr. with David Chanoff, *The Line of Fire: From Washington to the Gulf, the Politics and Battles of the New Military* (Simon & Schuster, 1993), pp. 264–69.

10. William Strunk Jr. and E. B. White, *The Elements of Style* (Macmillan, 1979), p. 23.

11. One widely used text in this area, albeit one with a quantitative bias, is Edith Stokey and Richard Zeckhauser, *A Primer for Policy Analysis* (W. W. Norton, 1978).

12. For some techniques in doing just this, see Richard E. Neustadt and Ernest R. May, *Thinking In Time: The Uses of History for Decision-Makers* (Free Press, 1986).

13. Daniel P. Moynihan, *The Politics of a Guaranteed Income: The Nixon Administration and the Family Assistance Plan* (Random House, 1973), p. 165.

14. Walter Isaacson, *Kissinger* (Simon & Schuster, 1992), p. 113.

15. I say this leaving open the question of whether what was decided by Justice Department officials at the time of the Waco incident was in fact the best course of action given what was known or might reasonably have been expected to be known at the time. See, for example, two articles in the *New York Times* by Stephen Labaton: "Report on Initial Raid on Cult Finds Officials Erred and Lied," October 1, 1993, pp. A1, A20, and "Reno Contradicted in New Report on Decision to Attack Waco Cult," October 9, 1993, pp. 1, 11.

16. See Cyrus Vance, *Hard Choices: Critical Years in America's Foreign Policy* (Simon & Schuster, 1983), pp. 408–13.

17. The text of Ritter's resignation letter is reprinted in the *Washington Times*, August 28, 1998, p. A12.

18. Shultz is quoted in *Newsweek,* August 3, 1989, p. 19.

19. For Haig's view, see Alexander M. Haig Jr., *Caveat: Realism, Reagan, and Foreign Policy* (Macmillan, 1984), pp. 303–16.

Chapter 4

1. John Gardiner, *On Leadership* (Free Press, 1990), p. 1.

2. William A. Cohen, *The Art of the Leader* (Englewood Cliffs, N.J.: Prentice Hall, 1990), p. 15.

3. Stephen R. Covey, *The 7 Habits of Highly Effective People* (Simon & Schuster/Fireside, 1989), p. 101.

4. Joe D. Batten, *Tough-Minded Leadership* (New York: American Management Association, 1989), p. 2.

5. Warren Bennis and Burt Nanus, *Leaders: The Strategies for Taking Charge* (Harper & Row, 1985), p. 21.

6. Peter F. Drucker, *Managing the Non-Profit Organization: Principles and Practices* (Harper Collins, 1990), p. 20.

7. L. William Seidman, *Full Faith and Credit: The Great S&L Debacle and Other Washington Sagas* (Times Books, 1993), p. 95.

8. The quotation is from an interview by Herman Nickel of W. Michael Blumenthal, entitled "Candid Reflections of a Businessman in Washington," that appeared in *Fortune,* January 29, 1979, p. 39.

9. Niccolo Machiavelli, *The Prince* (Chicago: Henry Regnery, 1963 ed.), p. 119.

10. Byron L. Johnson and Robert Ewegen, *B.S.: The Bureaucratic Syndrome* (Croton-on-Hudson, N.Y.: North River Press, 1982), p. 82.

11. A thoughtful short paper on the subject has been written by James Q. Wilson. See his "Thinking About Reorganization" (Washington, D.C.: Consortium for the Study of Intelligence, 1992).

12. Robert R. Reich, *Locked in the Cabinet* (Alfred A. Knopf, 1997), pp. 53–54.

13. I have drawn here on James MacGregor Burns, *Leadership* (Harper & Row, 1978), pp. 408–09, and on an unpublished "Policy Development Note" written by Richard Darman in 1980 and revised by Mark Moore in 1982 for the Kennedy School of Government.

14. Arthur M. Schlesinger Jr., *The Age of Roosevelt: Volume II: The Coming of the New Deal* (Boston: Houghton Mifflin, 1959), p. 528.

15. Excerpts of the report written by Richard H. Girgenti, New York State's director of Criminal Justice, on the August 1991 Crown Heights violence and official responses to it, can be found in the *New York Times,* July 21, 1993.

16. Richard E. Neustadt, *Presidential Power and the Modern Presidents: The Politics of Leadership from Roosevelt to Reagan* (Free Press, 1990), p. 28.

17. Mark H. McCormack, *What They Still Don't Teach You at Harvard Business School* (Bantam Books, 1989), p. 137.

18. Machiavelli, *The Prince*, pp. 90–97.

19. William G. Pagonis, *Moving Mountains: Lessons in Leadership and Logistics from the Gulf War* (Boston: Harvard Business School Press, 1992), pp. 185–87.

20. As quoted in Gordon R. Sullivan and Michael V. Harper, *Hope Is Not a Method: What Business Leaders Can Learn from America's Army* (Random House, 1996), p. 124.

21. Ann Reilly Dowd, "What Managers Can Learn from Manager Reagan," *Fortune*, September 15, 1986, p. 36.

22. Ann Reilly Dowd, "Learning from Reagan's Debacle," *Fortune*, April 27, 1987, pp. 169–72.

23. For an account of this reform, see Joseph A. Fernandez with John Underwood, *Tales Out of School: Joseph Fernandez's Crusade to Rescue American Education* (Boston: Little, Brown, 1993), pp. 148–60.

24. See, for example, Kathleen Sylvester, "Risk and the Culture of Innovation," *Governing*, October 1992.

25. Joseph Heller, *Good as Gold* (London: Jonathan Cape, 1979), p. 191.

26. For some useful advice on this and other nuts and bolts aspects of managing people in the public sector, see Jonathan Brock, *Managing People in Public Agencies: Personnel and Labor Relations* (Lanham, Md.: University Press of America, 1984).

Chapter 5

1. Peggy Noonan, *What I Saw at the Revolution: A Political Life in the Reagan Era* (Random House, 1990), p. 72.

2. James MacGregor Burns, *Leadership* (Harper & Row, 1978), p. 375.

3. Kemp's struggles within the Bush administration provide a case study of the problems that can be encountered in translating good ideas into policy. See Jason DeParle, "How Jack Kemp Lost the War on Poverty," *New York Times Magazine*, February 28, 1993.

4. Richard E. Neustadt, *Presidential Power and the Modern Presidents: The Politics of Leadership from Roosevelt to Reagan* (Free Press, 1990), p. 32.

5. These phrases are derived from two popular books on negotiations: *Getting to Yes: Negotiating Agreement without Giving In*, by Roger Fisher and William Ury (Viking Penguin, 1991); and *Getting Past No: Negotiating Your Way from Confrontation to Cooperation*, by William Ury (Bantam Books, 1993).

6. I owe this reference to *Leadership*, compiled and edited by William Safire and Leonard Safir (Simon & Schuster, 1990), p. 28.

7. See Bob Woodward, "The Secretary of Analysis," *Washington Post Magazine*, February 21, 1993, p. 29.

8. John Lewis (with Michael D'Orso), *Walking with the Wind: A Memoir of the Movement* (Simon & Schuster, 1998), pp. 209–10.

9. Harold Nicolson, *Diplomacy* (London: Oxford University Press, 1969), p. 25.

10. William Safire, *Before the Fall: An Inside View of the Pre-Watergate White House* (Garden City, N.Y.: Doubleday, 1975), p. 102.

11. George P. Shultz, *Turmoil and Triumph: My Years as Secretary of State* (Scribner's, 1993), pp. 107–08.

12. Wess Roberts, *Leadership Secrets of Attila the Hun* (New York: Warner Books, 1985), p. 57.

Chapter 6

1. James Q. Wilson, *Bureaucracy: What Government Agencies Do and Why They Do It* (Basic Books, 1989), p. 204.

2. Joseph A. Fernandez with John Underwood, *Tales Out of School: Joseph Fernandez's Crusade to Rescue American Education* (Boston: Little, Brown, 1993), pp. 195–96.

3. For a first-person account of someone who managed to alienate virtually all elements of both his East and West, see John Frohnmayer, *Leaving Town Alive: Confession of an Arts Warrior* (Boston: Houghton Mifflin, 1993). Frohnmayer is a textbook case in how not to work your compass to good effect.

4. Philip Selznick, *Leadership in Administration: A Sociological Interpretation* (Evanston, Ill.: Row Peterson, 1957), p. 145.

5. Christopher Matthews, *Hardball: How Politics Is Played—Told by One Who Knows the Game* (New York: Summit Books, 1988), p. 184.

6. See John R. Emshwiller, "Los Angeles Story: Peter Ueberroth Finds Fixing Riot-Torn City an Olympian Task," *Wall Street Journal*, April 5, 1993, pp. A1, A6.

7. Howard Kurtz, *Spin Cycle: Inside the Clinton Propaganda Machine* (Free Press, 1998), p. 92.

8. L. William Seidman, *Full Faith and Credit: The Great S&L Debacle and Other Washington Sagas* (New York: Times Books, 1993), pp. 248–49.

9. See Jack Nelson, "Many Clinton Goals in Peril, Panetta Warns," *Los Angeles Times*, April 27, 1993, pp. 1, 7.

10. Marlin Fitzwater, *Call the Briefing! Bush and Reagan, Sam and Helen; A Decade with the Presidents and Press* (New York: Times Books, 1995), p. 10.

11. William J. Crowe Jr., *The Line of Fire: From Washington to the Gulf, the Politics and Battles of the New Military* (Simon & Schuster, 1993), p. 231.

12. Mark Bisnow, *In the Shadow of the Dome: Chronicles of a Capitol Hill Aide* (New York: William Morrow, 1990), p. 56.

13. Richard Reeves, *President Kennedy: Profile of Power* (Simon & Schuster, 1993), p. 195.

14. Peggy Noonan, *What I Saw at the Revolution* (Random House, 1990), p. 58.

15. William Strunk Jr. and E. B. White, *The Elements of Style* (Macmillan, 1979), p. 69.

16. William Safire, *Before the Fall: An Inside View of the Pre-Watergate White House* (Garden City, N.Y.: Doubleday, 1975), p. 397.

Chapter 7

1. For background on this episode, see Bill McAllister and Barton Gellman, "Aspin Reverses Ban on Married Marines," *Washington Post*, August 12, 1993, pp. A1, A11; and Clifford Krauss, "Marine Leader Contritely Admits He Erred on 'Singles Only' Order," *New York Times*, August 13, 1993, pp. A1, A18. Typical of editorial opinion was "Marine Madness," *New York Times*, August 13, 1993, p. A26. For a rare voice in support of Mundy, see the op-ed by Bernard E. Trainor, "The Answer to a Marine Chaplain's Prayer," *New York Times*, August 13, 1993, p. A27.

LaVergne, TN USA
19 August 2009
155230LV00005B/1/A

9 780815 733539